LORD BURLINGTON'S TOWN ARCHITECTURE

Pamela D. Kingsbury

This book is published to coincide with the exhibition of the same name held at the RIBA Heinz Gallery, 26th January to 1st April 1995

RIBA Heinz Gallery 1995
Copyright ©1995 by Pamela D. Kingsbury
ISBN: 1 872911 40 4

Printed in England by Witley Press Ltd.

This catalogue is dedicated to my friends and colleagues in England for their generosity of spirit in sharing with me England's "Apollo of Arts", Lord Burlington

Funding for this catalogue was provided in large part by a grant from the Graham Foundation for Advanced Studies in the Fine Arts, Chicago.

The catalogue has also been made possible by the generosity of friends and institutions in Great Britain and the United States. I greatly appreciate the support of the Price R. and Flora A. Reid Foundation, John Phillip Kassebaum, Trustee, Wichita, Kansas, and the Drue Heinz Trust, Pittsburgh, Pennsylvania; the Idlewild Trust and the Paul Mellon Centre for Studies in British Art, London. A special word of thanks is extended to individual donors: Edith S. Bingham of Glenview, Kentucky, who gave me the impetus to start raising funds; Rowland and Eleanor Bingham Miller of Louisville, Kentucky; and my friend and former colleague at the Victoria and Albert Museum, Vera Kaden of Kingston, near Lewes, Sussex.

Contents

Foreword 6

Acknowledgments 8

Introduction 11

1 Burlington's Architectural Education 14

2 The Institutional Designs and Buildings 21

3 The Town Houses 59

Conclusion 87

Notes 89

Foreword by John Newman

It is twenty two years since the last exhibition devoted to Burlington. "Apollo of the Arts: Lord Burlington and his Circle", at the Nottingham University Art Gallery, celebrated the range of his involvement in the visual arts and in music. Pamela Kingsbury, in mounting the present exhibition, has a quite different concern, to illustrate Burlington's achievement in one major area of architectural design, his urban commissions. This narrowing of the focus vividly demonstrates his creativity and the fertility of his ideas within the pure and restrained style which he believed best represented the neo-antique ideal.

To the tidy-minded Richard Boyle, 3rd Earl of Burlington, has always presented a paradox. How could a peer of the realm, who had the ambition to steer the arts through his power and patronage, that is to say to become the virtuoso called for by the philosopher Shaftesbury, also practise as an architect? In Lord Chesterfield's view Burlington had demeaned himself by so doing, and the Duchess of Marlborough's satirical comments on the unfinished York Assembly Rooms, quoted by Dr Kingsbury, suggest that she thought him out of his depth in this role. In the present century much has been made of the involvement of William Kent, in particular at Chiswick and Holkham, and Burlington's design skills have been correspondingly underplayed. Yet, as Fiske Kimball pointed out as long ago as 1927, Burlington proudly signed drawings 'architectus'. On the foundation stone of Westminster School Dormitory too he was named as 'architect': and his skill as designer was so well known by 1730 that his fellow Yorkshire landowners invited him to be the architect of their proposed assembly rooms, after the death of that other local amateur architect, Sir William Wakefield. Once he had secured the commission, Burlington wrote to the directors of the assembly rooms in terms particularly revealing of the quasi-professional way he worked, in a letter quoted by Dr Kingsbury.

To judge from Alexander Pope's Epistle to Lord Burlington, published at the time the York Assembly Rooms design was being finalised, public buildings were his first concern, not the villas and country houses which are today most intimately associated with the Palladian movement.

Dr Kingsbury's exhibition reflects Pope's emphasis, for it concentrates on Burlington's designs for public architecture and puts them in the context of his other urban designs, and those for a handful of private houses. All the drawings exhibited here, though executed by professional draughtsmen working from Burlington's sketches and instructions, represent Burlington's own designs. The great series of designs for new Houses of Parliament, 1733-39, the commission which must have been viewed by Burlington as the greatest architectural opportunity of his lifetime, are attributable to Kent. So, although they must incorporate many of Burlington's ideas, they are omitted here.

The exhibition reveals Burlington's ability to take one type of public building after another – school dormitory, school and almshouse, hospital, assembly rooms – and reinterpret it with daring originality. He was able to do this, as Dr Kingsbury demonstrates, by exploiting his collection of Palladio's reconstruction drawings of Roman baths, perhaps the most impressive type of antique public building. In his town house designs too, he pays homage to his great master, in particular in the design for General Wade's celebrated house, a stone's throw from Burlington House itself.

Burlington's family connections may have helped him to win jobs but his social position certainly did not make it easier to get his designs built. He experienced the disappointment all too familiar to architects through the ages, of having schemes set aside, as at Chichester, or built in drastically altered form, as seems to have happened at Sevenoaks. Nor has he been fortunate in the survival of his executed urban works. Only the York Assembly Rooms, shorn of its façade, stands. Perhaps the most grievous loss is the Duke of Richmond's house in Whitehall, which must have been one of London's greatest Palladian mansions.

So the drawings in this exhibition are all the more precious, recording all too tantalisingly the ideas of one of the most original and influential of British architects.

Acknowledgments

Since the original gift in 1894 of the Burlington-Devonshire Collection of drawings, comprising 17 volumes of Palladio's drawings, a large array of drawings by Inigo Jones and his assistant, John Webb, and drawings by Lord Burlington and his chief draughtsman, Henry Flitcroft, and others, the Drawings Collection of the Royal Institute of British Architects has grown to become the outstanding repository of Palladian and Neo-Palladian drawings. It is, therefore, very appropriate to celebrate the tricentenary of Burlington's birth with an exhibition devoted to Lord Burlington's Palladian town architecture at the RIBA Heinz Gallery.

This publication and the accompanying exhibition would not have been possible without the dedication of the staff of the RIBA Drawings Collection. To Jill Lever, Curator, goes my deep appreciation and gratitude for her unflagging determination to hold this exhibition. I am particularly grateful to Dr Neil Bingham, the coordinator of the exhibition, who faithfully and with good humour answered all my numerous questions and pleas for help. My gratitude also goes to their colleagues: Tim Knox, for his knowledgeable advice concerning General Wade's house and collection; Charlotte Podro and Sian Williams, for all the care and conservation of the exhibition drawings; Andrew Norris, for his excellent installation of the exhibition; and Jane Preger, an old friend from my student days at the RIBA Drawings Collection, for her handsome catalogue design.

I extend a very special debt of gratitude to my friend and colleague Dr Gordon Higgott for reading and criticising my manuscript, for which, of course, I assume full responsibility; and to John Newman, who through these many years has guided and encouraged me in my research into Burlington's architecture.

For their kind assistance I would like to thank the Trustees of the Chatsworth Settlement, Peter Day and his staff at Chatsworth House; Mr Stanley-Morgan; the West Yorkshire Archive Service; the Dean and Chapter of Westminster Abbey, and especially

Dr Richard Mortimer, Keeper of the Muniments; the Trustees of Westminster School, and in particular Peter Holmes, Archivist; Mike Evans, National Monuments Record, for his efficient service; Jane Clark and Stephen Dodgson for assistance with research on General Wade; and David Alexander for his help with the York Assembly Rooms. In the United States, I wish to extend my gratitude to Joseph Connors of Columbia University, New York City; to Kevin Harrington of the Illinois Institute of Technology, Chicago; to Earl E. Rosenthal of the University of Chicago; and to Howard W. Ellington, Executive Director of the Kansas Cultural Trust, Wichita, Kansas.

ACKNOWLEDGMENTS FOR ILLUSTRATIONS

For permission to reproduce the following illustrations I would like to thank: Bodleian Library, Oxford, 9, 10,13,15, 33; British Library, 47; British Museum, 60, 72, 77; Harris Museum and Art Gallery, Preston, 1; Lord Bishop of London, the Church Commissioners for England and the Courtauld Institute of Art, 48; Mr Stanley Morgan, 54; National Monuments Record, 28, 41, 55, 59, 63; National Portrait Gallery Archives, 23; RIBA Drawings Collection, 12, 14, 17, 19, 20, 24, 25, 36, 37, 49, 50, 51, 52, 57, 58, 61, 62, 64, 65, 70, 71, 73, 74, 75, 76; Trustees of the Chatsworth Settlement, 6, 27, 29, 30, 31, 32, 34, 38, 45, 46, 53, 66, 67; West Yorkshire Archive Service, 56; York City Art Gallery, 44; John Davis, 16. The following illustrations are taken from publications: *Eboracum*, 35; *The Designs of Inigo Jones*, 21; John Rocque, *Plan of the Garden and Estate at Chiswick*, 5; *I Quattro Libri*, 22, 42; *Vitruvius Britannicus*, 2, 3, 4. Photographs by the author: 7, 8, 11, 18, 26, 39, 40, 43, 69.

Front cover: Garden elevation of General Wade's house, 1723
Back cover: Front elevation of First Design for the Chichester Council House, 1730

1
Portrait of Lord and
Lady Burlington, 1723,
by William Aikman

Introduction

When one thinks about the architecture of Richard Boyle, the 3rd Earl of Burlington and the 4th Earl of Cork (1694-1753), buildings set in a bucolic country landscape come immediately to mind.[1] (Fig. 1) Foremost among these, and lying at the heart of his architecture, is Burlington's suburban villa on the Thames at Chiswick, six miles west of Hyde Park Corner. Acting in a dual capacity as his own client and architect, Burlington designed a villa for himself, gardens, buildings for the gardens, and other related structures. Indeed, over half of his architecture, the built as well as the unbuilt, is devoted to buildings in a country ambience. But this should not obscure the fact that he also designed a number of buildings for the cities and towns, from London, his major focus of attention, to Chichester, Sevenoaks, York, and the village of Bishop Burton. With the exception of religious buildings, he executed designs for some of the most important building types of the first half of the eighteenth century: assembly rooms, a council house, dormitory, hospital, and school and almshouses.

Burlington's emergence as an architect came at a time of great change and innovation in the arts. By the second decade of the century, England was experiencing a resurgence of interest in the Italian classical tradition that swept through the world of literature, the visual arts, and the performing arts of music and opera. Architecture, because of its highly visible, public nature, was in the forefront of these changes. Although Italy was considered to be the guiding spirit of the classical tradition, it was not primarily the classical world of Rome that served as the model, as it did for literature, but, rather, it was the Italian Renaissance and its permutations that defined the standards to be followed. Some may ascribe this momentous shift in taste and style to a reaction to the Baroque exuberance of Wren, Hawksmoor, and Vanbrugh. Still others may see this classical revival as a creation of the Whig aristocracy, who, after the death of Queen Anne in 1714, were seeking to control not only the government but also the social and cultural life of the country. But, for whatever reason, English architecture was returning to its classical heritage, established in the seventeenth century by Inigo Jones (1573-1652), as Surveyor of the King's Works and chief architect to the Stuart courts of James I and Charles I.

For architecture, the cornerstone and chief manifesto of the classical revival was Colen Campbell's three-volume *magnum opus, Vitruvius Britannicus, or The British Architect.* In the introduction to the first volume, published in 1715, Campbell sets the parameters of the movement and establishes the canonical guides for England's return to the classical fold. After acknowledging his debt "to those Restorers of Architecture," that is, Italian architects such as Bramante, Raphael, and Michelangelo, he selects "the great Palladio" as one of the guiding spirits of the classical revival, who "has exceeded all that were gone before him, and surpass'd his Contemporaries," who rivals "most of the Ancients," and who has arrived at "a *Ne plus ultra* of his Art."[2] For the other guiding spirit, Campbell chose his fellow countryman "the Famous Inigo Jones," who, by the example of his architecture, had "out-done all that went before."[3]

Among his fellow architects, Burlington was in an exceptional position to make a significant contribution to the classical revival. Unlike such major architects as Campbell, Gibbs, and Leoni, who were required to make their living as architects, Burlington had wealth and social position and could make architecture his avocation and not his vocation. His commitment to architecture was not mitigated by his "amateur" status. On the contrary, his wealth and social position permitted him to design without compromising his ideals and, in many instances, without regard for client demands and the economic restrictions and limitations normally imposed upon architects. With his wealth and passion for architecture he was able to amass the finest collection of architectural drawings in England, if not in Europe. It consisted of the largest single corpus of Palladio's drawings of his own architecture and his reconstructions of the ancient baths and other Roman monuments, as well as the architectural drawings of Inigo Jones and John Webb. This collection was equalled in importance only by George Clarke's collection of architectural drawings by Jones, Webb, and others at Oxford.[4] Supplementing his drawings collection was an equally magnificent architectural library, scholarly in nature and consisting of virtually all the published editions of architectural treatises and texts, beginning with a mid-fifteenth century incunabulum on vellum of Vitruvius's *Ten Books of Architecture*.[5] With an architectural career that spanned more than twenty years and aided by his drawings collection and architectural library, Burlington became the major advocate and primary arbiter of the Palladian phase of the classical revival. In so doing, he accepted the parameters defined by Campbell for the rebirth of the classical tradition and, like him, chose Palladio and Jones as his mentors. Palladio was indispensable to Burlington. He was his cicerone to the classical tradition, offering a clear and succinct presentation of his architectural principles in his own architecture and his drawings of classical Roman architecture, but above all in his treatise, *I Quattro Libri*, in which his architecture and that of Rome were analysed and illustrated. On the other hand, Burlington looked with a critical eye to Jones as his guide to the classical tradition in England, analysing Jones's architecture for its classical precedents and its usefulness. Working according to these precedents, Burlington fashioned an architecture that was lucid and didactic in character, stark in its application of architectural detailing, and possessed of an internal logic that led from Palladio and Jones to classical Rome and Vitruvius.

For all the influence Burlington wielded during his lifetime in architecture and in the arts in general, it is surprising that his architectural production was quite small. Excluding interior alterations, some bridges and gates, and an assortment of garden buildings, only ten institutional buildings and residences Burlington designed were erected. His clients or patrons, if these terms are applicable in his case, constituted a closely knit group consisting of himself, his family, and his friends. Despite this small architectural oeuvre, his designs, built and unbuilt, for the emerging English urban scene form an important and much neglected aspect of his architecture. They span his entire architectural career from Lord Mountrath's town house, an early work of *c.*1721, to an addition to the York Assembly Rooms of 1735 during the twilight of his career.

Chapter 1

BURLINGTON'S ARCHITECTURAL EDUCATION

Burlington probably did not become an architect in his own right until his return from a second trip to Italy late in 1719. Unlike his first sojourn in Italy, which culminated his year-long Grand Tour of 1714-15, his second Italian trip, begun in August 1719, was undertaken to study the architecture of Andrea Palladio in Vicenza, in the surrounding countryside of the Veneto, and in Venice. In contrast to his fellow countrymen William Kent and Thomas Coke, who were living in Italy during Burlington's Grand Tour and traveled extensively to study Italian architecture, Burlington evinced no interest.[1] His two consuming passions on the Grand Tour were music and the collecting of paintings. From Brussels, the first major stop of any duration on the Grand Tour to Rome, where he spent the autumn and winter of 1714-15, to Florence, Venice, and finally to Paris in the spring of 1715, Burlington indulged his passion for collecting by the purchase of paintings. As Massingberd, an earnest patron of Kent, wrote in a letter to him in Rome, "[M]y Ld Burlington is coming full of money."[2] The focus of his picture collecting was the Italian school, now termed the Baroque, and some of its leading masters, Annibale Carracci, Domenichino, and Cortona, and the masters of the succeeding generation, led by Carlo Maratta and his followers Giordano and Chiari. Music was the other great passion of Burlington's Grand Tour, and in Italy and Paris he rented harpsichords for his lodgings, engaged musicians to play for him, and attended the opera. So taken was he with Italian music that in Rome he added the string players Pietro and Prospero Castruzzi and Filippo Amadei to his entourage for his homeward journey.

The four years between his two Italian sojourns served as the time for Burlington's architectural apprenticeship at Burlington House under the guidance of Colen Campbell, who had replaced James Gibbs as the architect in charge, and at his suburban estate at Chiswick. In addition to this firsthand experience, he must have immersed himself in reading architectural treatises and texts. From the very few scraps of information gleaned from correspondence and in the poetry of John Gay and Alexander Pope, it would seem that Burlington's initial foray into architecture came in the design and laying out of a new garden at Chiswick. Although he is described as having "a good Taste in Painting and Gardening,"[3] it is unlikely that he possessed the knowledge, experience, or technical skills to design and lay out a formal garden. In all probability, he was assisted by Charles Bridgeman, who, according to Horace Walpole, was responsible for the "phlegmatic plantations . . . at the back of the house at Chiswick."[4] Subject to Burlington's approval, Bridgeman superimposed a *patte d'oie* onto the avenues and structure of the formal garden to the north of the Jacobean House.

During this period, Burlington probably did not possess the knowledge or experience to design buildings. Despite Campbell's assertion that the *Casina* or *Bagno*, as he termed the building that was to be situated at the terminus of the west *alleé* of the *patte d'oie*, was "the First Essay of my Lordship's Happy Invention,"[5] this garden building has much more in common with Campbell's own architecture than with the buildings Burlington subsequently designed for the garden. The

2
The *Casina*, attributed to Colen Campbell

3
The Great Gate,
Burlington House,
Piccadilly, London,
Colen Campbell

4
Front elevation of
Burlington House,
Colen Campbell

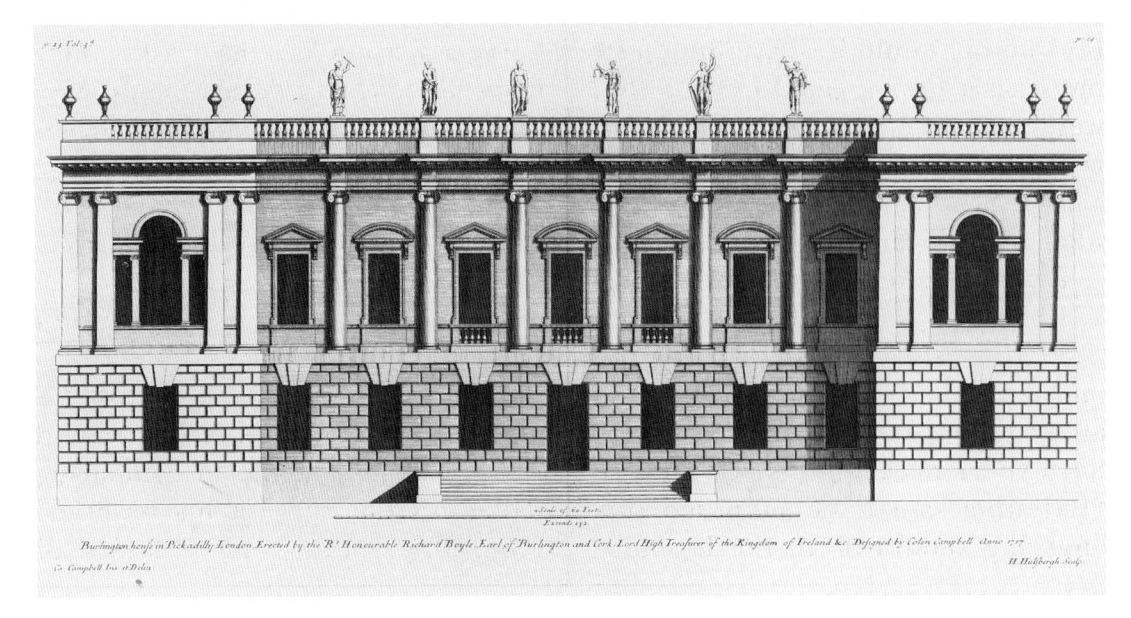

ground-floor elevation of the *Casina* is a stripped-down version of Campbell's Great Gate at Burlington House, and the first-floor with its Serliana window recalls the first-floor end bays on the front elevation of Burlington House. (Figs. 2, 3 & 4) Given Campbell's penchant to flatter his clients in *Vitruvius Britannicus*, he may well have been responsible for the design of the *Casina* but, to win favour with his young patron, may have given him credit for the garden building. The other garden building erected at the same time as the *Casina* was a small, domed, tetrastyle garden seat at the end of the central *alleé* of the *patte d'oie*. (Fig. 5) Like the *Casina*, this building has far more in common with the architecture of James Gibbs than with the garden buildings Burlington would design after 1719. Since both Campbell and Gibbs were working in the garden in 1719, they were probably the designers of the two garden buildings, and not Burlington, who, at this point, was a mere novice.

Burlington's return to Italy in August 1719 was an acknowledgment of his need to possess a visual as well as intellectual understanding of Palladio's architecture. As Roger Pratt wrote of his experiences on the Continent, "[N]either can it be supposed that anything should be in the Intellect, which was never in the senses"[6] and "True it is that a man may receive some helps upon a most diligent study from those excellent, and most exact designs of Palladio, Freart, Scamozzi, and some few others, yet never having seen anything in its full proportions, it is not to be thought that he can conceive of them as he ought."[7] Burlington's personal study of Palladio's architecture, which was hampered by the most torrential rains in three hundred years,[8] was an exercise in comparing Palladio's theory with his practice. From this study came a series of

5
The tetrastyle temple in the garden at Chiswick, attributed to James Gibbs, from John Rocque's *Plan of the Garden Villa and Estate at Chiswick*, 1736

annotations that he recorded in a specially prepared 1601 edition of Palladio's *I Quattro Libri*, the same edition that Jones used on his famous 1613-14 tour of Italy. (Fig. 6) On the interleaved pages in Book II dealing with Palladio's architecture, Burlington recorded his impressions and analyses of three of Palladio's most important Vicentine palaces, the palazzi Chiericati, Porto, and Thiene, and his two most outstanding suburban villas, La Rotonda on the outskirts of Vicenza and Malcontenta on the banks of the Brenta, where it empties into the Lagoon at Venice. And on the interleaved page between the title page and the prolegomenon, he recorded eight observations about Palladio's great Benedictine church of San Giorgio Maggiore in Venice, a building not included in his treatise.[9] These annotations, although small in number and aphoristic in character, provide a wealth of information and offer insights into Burlington's architectural theory and practice that neither his extant buildings nor his drawings can provide.

Of equal importance to his development as an architect, and a major factor in determining the character of his architecture, was Burlington's acquisition of a cache of Palladio's drawings of Roman architecture that he saw at the Villa Maser and subsequently purchased in Venice.[10] Among these are Palladio's reconstructions of the Roman baths, a large selection of which Burlington eventually published at his own expense.[11] Shortly after his return to London, he began to add to his architectural drawings collection. On 4 May 1720, he paid John Talman, the son of the architect William Talman, for "a Book of Designes & Plans etc. by Inigo Jones."[12] The following spring on 4 April 1721, he purchased from Talman "a Parcell of Architectonical Designes and Drawings by Palladio."[13] With these three purchases, Burlington now possessed a veritable documented history of the classical tradition as it pertained to Italy and England. Having studied Palladio's architecture personally and having at his fingertips a virtual museum of architecture on paper, Burlington struck out on his own as an architect. His initial foray into the field probably occurred in his new garden at Chiswick, where, by 1724, he had designed and erected three garden buildings that in varying degrees are dependent upon the architecture and architectural drawings of Palladio and Jones.[14]

At the end of the east *alleé* of the *patte d'oie*, he erected a small garden building that will be referred to as the Rustic *Aedicule*. This diminutive building owed its appearance and defining characteristics to Burlington's study of Jones's Oatlands Palace vineyard gate and to his admiration for Palladio's Palazzo Thiene. (Fig. 7) On the western edge of the estate were erected two other garden buildings within their own garden enclosures. Facing west and overlooking an

6 (Facing page)
Title page of Burlington's copy of Palladio's *I Quattro Libri Dell'Architettura*, 1601

7
The Rustic Aedicule in the Garden at Chiswick, Lord Burlington, c.1720-24

8
The Ionic Temple in the Orange Tree Garden at Chiswick, Lord Burlington, c. 1720-24

apsidal pool was a three-bay building that will be referred to as the Tuscan Banqueting House and whose most noteworthy feature was its distyle *in antis* Tuscan porch fashioned after the Tuscan portico of Jones's St. Paul's Church, Covent Garden. Just to the south lay the tetrastyle Ionic Temple, a miniature version of the Pantheon, with its portico patterned after that of the Temple of Fortuna Virilis. The Ionic Temple looks down upon a garden in the shape of three concentric circles, or so-called "amphitheatre," upon which were placed tubs of orange trees during the summer months. At the center of the garden is a circular pool, a stone obelisk on a tall pedestal rising from it.[15] (Fig. 8)

Simultaneously with the work in the garden at Chiswick, Burlington undertook the task of remodeling the Wiltshire country house of Tottenham Park for his brother-in-law, Charles, Lord Bruce, from 1721 onward. A year later, as "Architectus," Burlington laid the foundation stone for the Westminster school dormitory, the first in a series of institutional buildings that would culminate in his greatest institutional achievement, the York Assembly Rooms, in the early 1730s.

Chapter 2

The Institutional Designs and Buildings

Westminster Dormitory

Burlington was not the first choice as architect of the Westminster Dormitory; nor would he have received the job had it not been for an acrimonious, litigious thirteen-year controversy that enabled him to step in at the last moment. In 1708, Sir Edward Hannes, a Westminster graduate and physician to Queen Anne, bequeathed £1,000 to build a new dormitory for the Queen's Scholars. Hannes's will directed that the Dean and Chapter of Westminster select the appropriate site for the new dormitory and, furthermore, consult two Westminster graduates, Christopher Wren, (1632-1723) Surveyor of the King's Works, and the amateur architect Henry Aldrich, Dean of Corpus Christi, Oxford.[1] Over the next thirteen years, the Dean and Chapter engaged in a heated debate over whether to remodel the old dormitory, housed in a medieval granary located on the western edge of the Dean's Yard, or to build a new one. Francis Atterbury, appointed Dean of Westminster in 1713, soon persuaded his colleagues to erect a new dormitory and recommended a site occupied by an orchard in the College Garden. (Fig. 9) Another heated debate then ensued over the advisibility of this site for the new dormitory, with the final decision being made by the House of Lords,

9
Engraving of *A General Plan of the Common Garden, Dean's Yard and the Buildings Contiguous Thereto*, 1719, William Dickinson

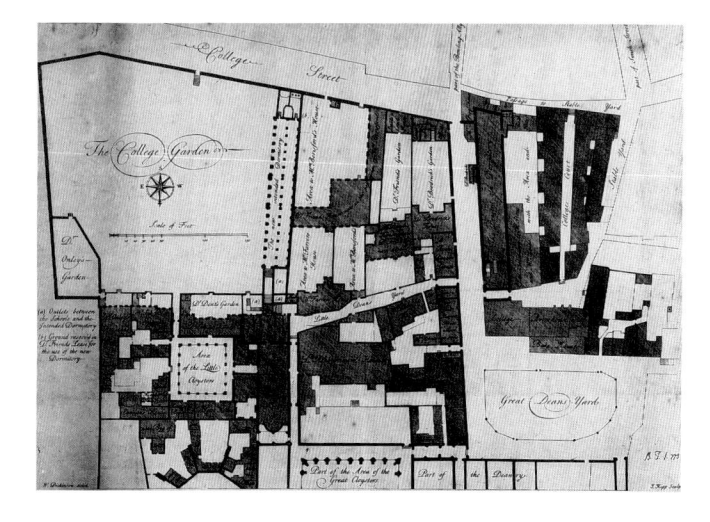

21

10
Ground plan and front elevation of Westminster Dormitory, 1713/14, William Dickinson

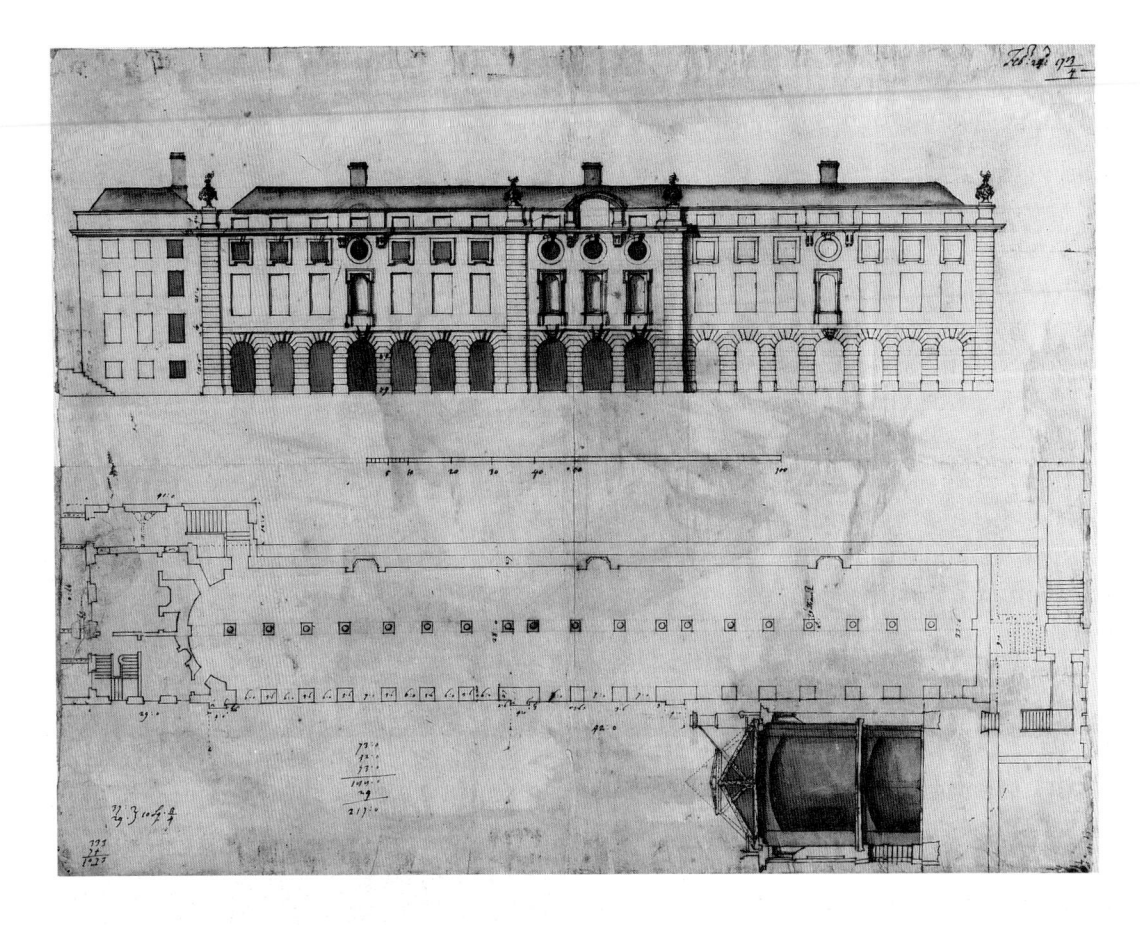

who, on 16 May 1721, decreed that it be erected in the College Garden.[2] Although Wren was officially the architect of record, he delegated the responsibility of designing the dormitory to William Dickinson (c.1671-1725), Surveyor to the Dean and Chapter of Westminster. When Atterbury became Dean, all Dickinson's efforts were directed towards a new design for the College Garden, which preoccupied him from 1714 to 1721. The design he submitted is a grand Baroque dormitory, with a strong vertical thrust, arcaded ground floor, and giant pilasters terminating the corners and defining the three central bays, which have ornately decorated occuli and blind windows with niches in them. (Fig. 10) Then events changed once again and not to the advantage of Wren and Dickinson. At some point shortly before, during, or after the House of Lords decreed the College Garden as the site for the new dormitory, Burlington replaced Wren and Dickinson as architect. Why this change occurred and who was responsible for it have remained a mystery to this day. Certainly, to change architects at such a late date could not have occurred without the approval and support of Dean Francis Atterbury, the driving force behind erecting the new dormitory in the College Garden. But it would take more than Atterbury to put forward someone from outside the precincts of Westminster Abbey and such a youthful, untried architect as Burlington. In all likelihood, Burlington obtained the position with the help of his uncle, Henry Boyle, Lord Carleton (d.1725), a powerful political figure and a Westminster graduate. As a Member of Parliament, Carleton held various offices, such as Chancellor of the Exchequer under Queen Anne and, from 1721, President of the Council under Walpole. (Fig. 11) Aiding Carleton might have been another Westminster graduate and a relative, Henry Boyle, first Earl of Shannon, who was to become the manager of Burlington's estates in Ireland.[3] In concert with Atterbury, these two men probably wielded enough power to convince the Chapter to dispense with the services of Wren and Dickinson and to start afresh with Burlington, whose dormitory design was in the avant-garde and offered a new vision for the future of the school.

For a short period of time before Burlington laid the foundation stone for the new dormitory in April 1722,[4] Dickinson struggled to respond to his

11
Portrait of Henry Boyle, Lord Carleton, 1740, engraved by Jacob Houbraken after Godfrey Kneller

12
Front elevation of
Westminster Dormitory,
c.1722, Lord Burlington

13
Front Elevation of
Westminster Dormitory,
1721, William Dickinson

rival's design with revised schemes that emulated Burlington's. Prominent among these revisions was Dickinson's stripped-down version of his Baroque dormitory design, devoid of decorative detailing except for a subdued Baroque exuberance in the three central bays of the elevation. (Figs. 12 & 13)

None of Burlington's drawings for his dormitory have survived, but we do have a series of four drawings by Henry Flitcroft (1697-1769), Burlington's chief draughtsman. (Fig. 14) According to the legend, Flitcroft came to Burlington's attention after falling from a scaffold while working as a joiner's apprentice at Burlington House.[5] He was probably working for

Burlington by 1720, first at Chiswick and then doing draughting work at Tottenham Park before moving on to the Westminster project. Flitcroft was very much Burlington's alter ego, turning his rough sketches and first thoughts into finished, highly polished drawings with a clarity and precision that perfectly complemented Burlington's architectural aesthetic. The design Burlington presented and the one that won over Dickinson's effort to resist it is an austere two-and-a-half-storey, arcaded building located on the western periphery of the College Garden with its rear wall abutting the prebendal residences to the west and its arcaded front elevation facing east onto the College Garden. (Fig. 9) The arcaded ground floor, intended to facilitate easy passage through the building and out into the College Garden, is defined by fifteen arches and was designed to have fifteen niches on the rear wall for statues. The first floor has niches in place of windows surmounted by alternating triangular and segmental pediments. Two-thirds of the first floor consists of sleeping quarters for the boys, with two fireplaces in the rear wall. The remaining third is reserved for the Second Masters.[6] (Fig. 15) Above, the mezzanine with square clerestory windows provides light for the sleeping quarters below. The dormitory was clad in Bath stone and is apparently an early example of its use on a London building.[7] The construction of the dormitory moved slowly, mired in disputes about workmen's wages that both the Chapter and Burlington failed to pay. Finally, seven years after Burlington laid the foundation stone for the dormitory, it was occupied in 1729.

Burlington's dormitory, still standing today and glowing from a recent cleaning, is as simple in its design as it is revolutionary in its

14 Portrait of Henry Flitcroft, c.1740, attributed to Bartholomew Dandridge

15
Ground and first floor plans and elevation for Westminster Dormitory, c 1722, Lord Burlington

outlook. (Fig. 16) The elevation of the dormitory is defined by Palladio's Ionic order as he applied it to an arcade in his treatise.[8] Absent from the elevation are engaged columns and pilasters that typify most buildings of the period. In their place is Palladio's Ionic order stringently applied to the arcades and fenestration and nowhere else. The culminating stroke is the boldly projecting Ionic cornice, also from Palladio's Ionic order and a subtle evocation of the absence of columns or pilasters on this astylar facade.

The arcaded building was a type traditionally used for dormitories and ranges of houses, but an astylar elevation of such uncompromising austerity was unique to English architecture. What were its origins? Certainly, Jones's arcaded "piazzas" enclosing Covent Garden, with their ashlar arcades, giant Tuscan pilasters the height of the first and mezzanine

16
Westminster Dormitory

storeys, and dormers in the roof, were not the direct sources of inspiration for Burlington. Nor was the Thames-side elevation of Jones's Somerset House, with its ashlar arcade and giant Corinthian pilasters dominating the first and mezzanine storeys. Not even the classically advanced Peckwater Quadrangle by Henry Aldrich (1706-14) at Christ Church, Oxford, with its ashlar ground floor, giant Ionic pilasters dominating the first and mezzanine storeys, and a pediment crowning the five central bays, would have appealed to Burlington. These facades would have seemed to him cluttered and confused, and entirely out of keeping with his concepts of classical architecture.

In all probability, the astylar treatment of his dormitory elevation is the result of Burlington's study of Palladio's reconstructions of the Roman baths. In his drawings, Palladio presented the elevations of the Roman baths stripped down to their masonry massing, with an emphasis on simple geometric shapes and unadorned

27

17
Henry Flitcroft's copy of
Andrea Palladio's
drawing of the Reconstruction of the Baths of
Agrippa, c.1550s

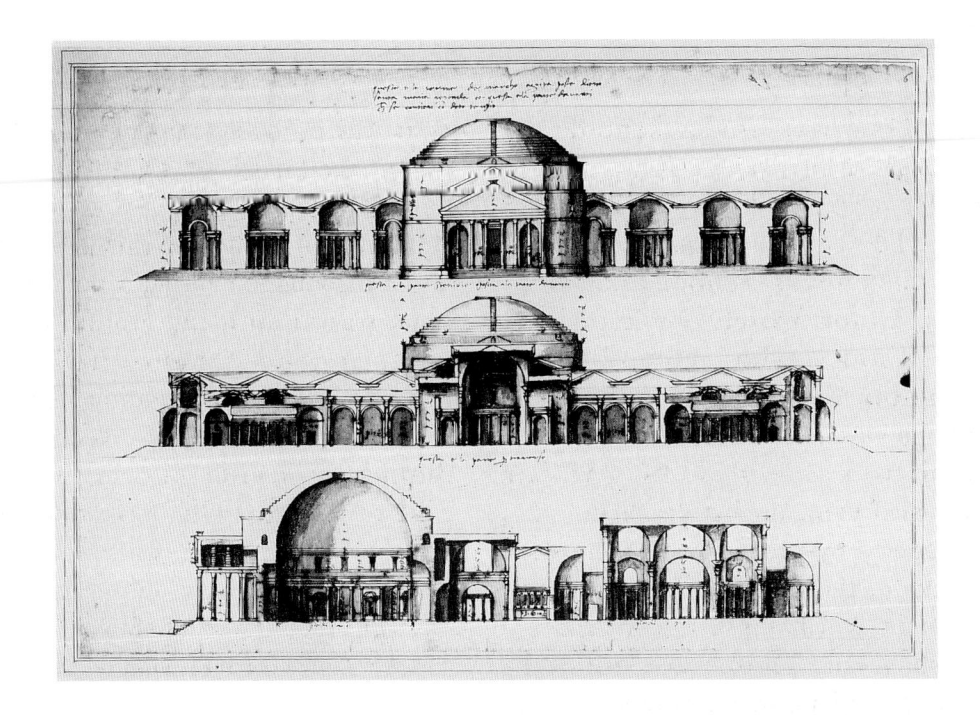

18
Palladio's cloister at San
Giorgio Maggiore,
Venice

surfaces. (Fig. 17) To reaffirm the lessons he had learned from a study of these drawings, Burlington examined another type of dormitory, Palladio's cloister at San Giorgio Maggiore, about which he recorded his impression.[9] Pairs of Ionic columns on the arcaded ground floor lead to a first floor defined by pedimented Ionic windows whose members are reduced to a bare minimum, with only a remnant of the column represented by right-angle pilasters in the corners supporting a block cornice. (Fig. 18)

Sevenoaks School and Almshouses Design

The next two designs did not have a life of their own beyond the draughting

28

table. One was for a school and almshouses in Sevenoaks, Kent, and the other for a council house in Chichester, Sussex. The earliest of the two projects is the Sevenoaks School and Almshouses. Unfortunately, we know very little about who commissioned Burlington and why the complex of buildings was never erected. Sevenoaks School was founded by William Sevenoaks, who, on his death in 1432, left property by the Thames in the City of London, the income from which was to be used to establish and maintain a free school and almshouses, admitting both rich and poor. Sevenoaks, a man of humble origins, rose in the City to become a successful merchant, Member of Parliament, and Mayor of the City of London. Among his many achievements was the establishment of the town of Sevenoaks, where the school was to be erected after his death.[10]

By 1721, the school building and almshouses were in a "very ruinous and decayed" state.[11] A year later, the Crown offered to buy the Thames riverside property in order to build a new Customs House. After the House of Lords approved the sale in 1724, the school Corporation, having decided to use the money for a new school and almshouses, approached Burlington about a design.[12]

It was probably Elijah Fenton (1683-1730), headmaster of Sevenoaks School from 1706 to c.1711, who asked Burlington to design the new school and almshouses. Fenton, a poet of some note, was in an ideal position to speak to Burlington, for they had mutual friends. Prior to his headmastership at Sevenoaks, Fenton was secretary to Burlington's cousin, Charles Boyle, the Earl of Orrery, who was educated at Sevenoaks. Fenton was also a personal friend of Alexander Pope and participated in translating several chapters of Homer's *Odyssey* for him.[13]

One source of information we have about the project is two of Burlington's drawings, of the floor plan of the first storey and the elevation of the school, and three bays of one of the almshouse wings. (Figs. 19 & 20) Another document is an engraving in Kent's *The Designs of Inigo Jones* that depicts the floor plan and elevation of the school and almshouses.[14] (Fig. 21) Unlike the old school and almshouses, which were three separate buildings located next to the main road of Sevenoaks,[15] Burlington designed one large complex, with the school at the centre and the almshouses flanking it.[16]

The complex was vast, measuring 565 feet in length, the almshouses having twenty bays and the school

19
First-floor plan of
Sevenoaks School,
c.1724, Lord Burlington

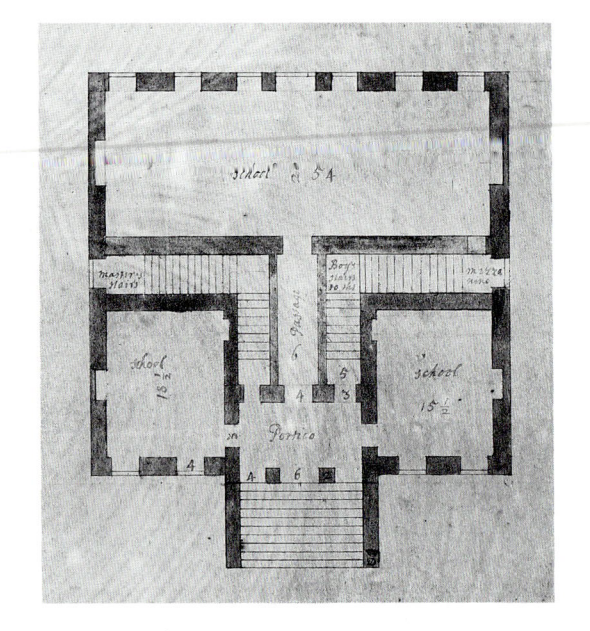

20
Elevation of Sevenoaks
School and Almshouses,
c.1724, Lord Burlington

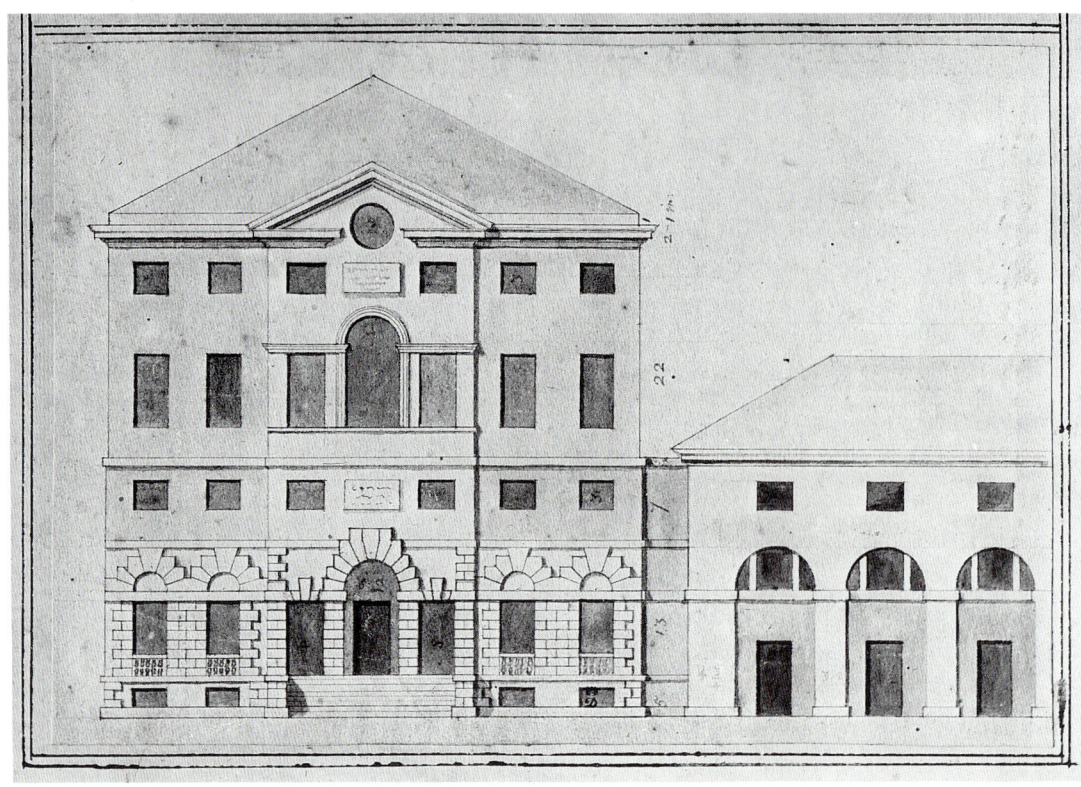

seven. Presumably, this complex was intended to be set back from the road, but close enough to make a visible statement about the relationship between free school education and Burlington's ideals concerning classical architecture. The school was to be very high, virtually 50 feet from the ground to the soffit of the roof, and the elevation gives the impression that Burlington simply multiplied storeys and mezzanines until the desired height was reached. Nevertheless, the school elevation contains several architectural elements that are staples of his architectural vocabulary. The first floor, raised on a half basement and faced with ashlar masonry, has a Serliana entrance flanked by secondary entrances in the form of double squares (6' x 12'), a standard practice of the day.[17] Inside the central entrance, there are classrooms on the left and right, and a long, narrow hall leads straight ahead to the largest classroom, which occupies half the first floor. The flanking entrances lead to a pair of staircases: on the left to the "Masters Stairs" and on the right to the "Boys Stairs." Above the first floor are two mezzanines, defined by double-square windows and between them a second storey dominated by a Serliana window. (Figs. 19 & 20)

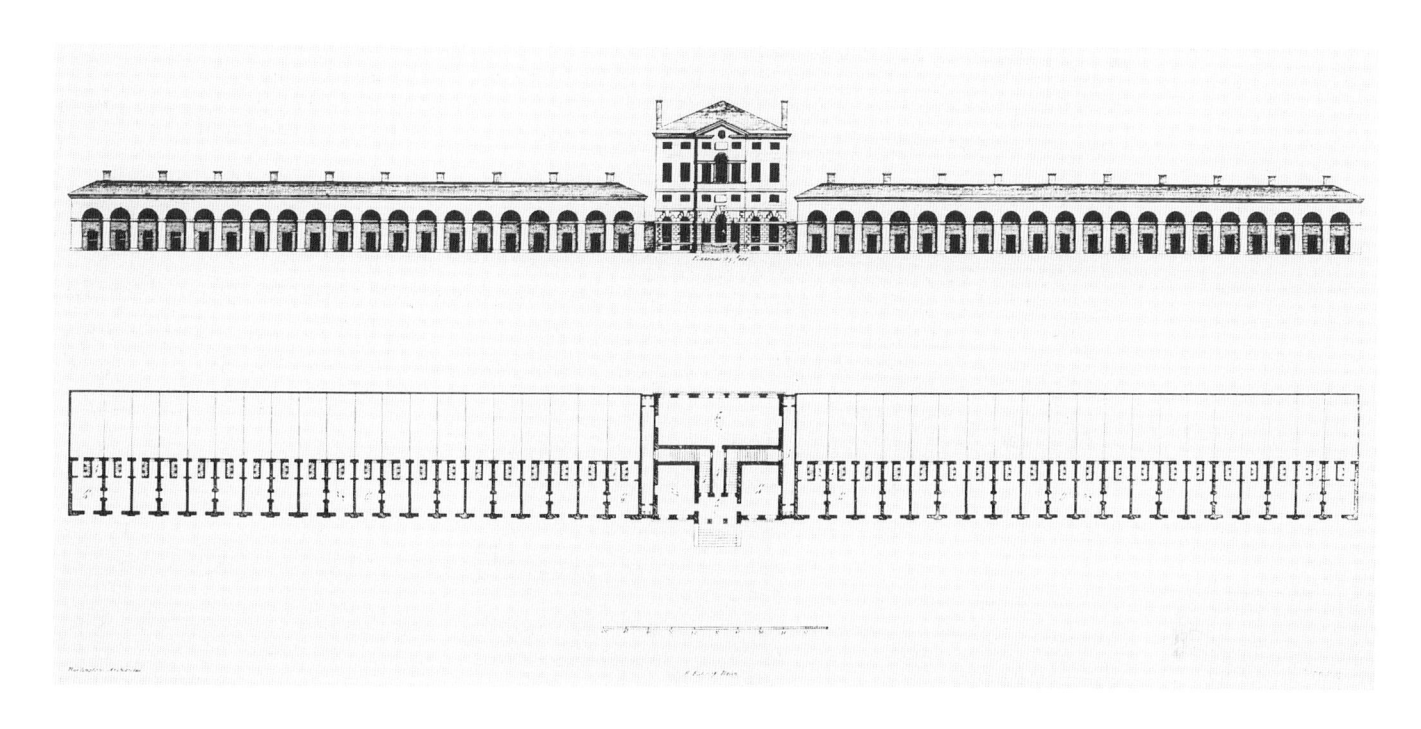

The great problem with Burlington's two drawings, and a problem that is not resolved by the engraving of the school and almshouses, is the location of the sleeping quarters for the students and masters. Burlington's drawing of the first-floor plan suggests that these were to be located on the second floor, the masters perhaps occupying the central three bays with the Serliana window and the students on either side. It does not seem feasible, however, that the

21
Ground-floor plan and elevation of Sevenoaks School and Almshouses, 1727, Lord Burlington

mezzanines were used as sleeping quarters; rather, they probably were not true mezzanines but a continuation of the first and second floors, with clerestory windows illuminating the sleeping quarters and classrooms below them. (Figs. 19 & 20)

The wings of the almshouses are twenty bays long and seem to stretch into infinity. Although the wings give the impression of being arcaded, they are not; each arcade arch is walled and provided with a door. As depicted in the engraving, the rooms of the almshouses were spacious. The ground floor has a fireplace, an alcove created by the stairs leading to the bedroom, and a window looking upon a garden plot that runs the depth of the school. (Fig. 21) From an architectural point of view, the most distinctive feature of the almshouses is the presence of thermal windows above each entrance. This type of window, its large openings permitting a generous amount of natural light, is derived from Palladio's reconstructions of the

22
Plan and elevation of the Villa Emo, Andrea Palladio

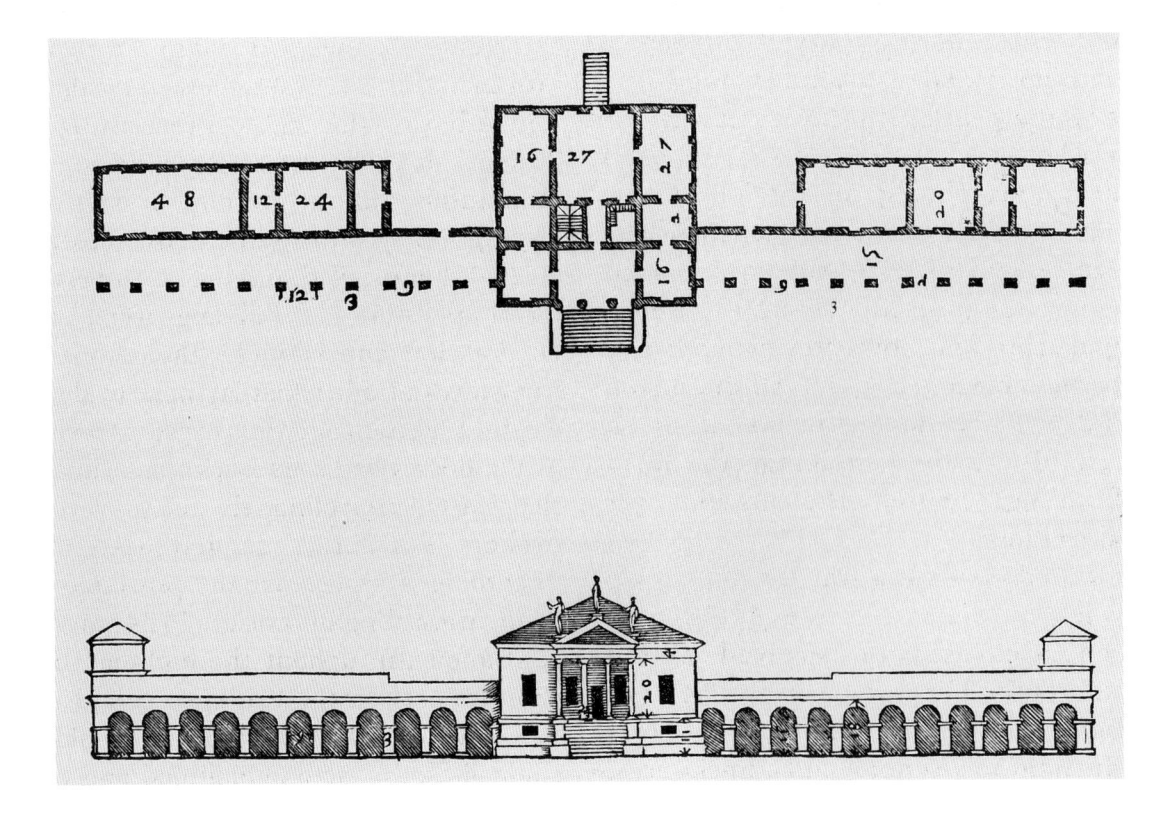

Roman baths. Like the Serliana window, it is one of the signature pieces of Burlington's architecture and is displayed prominently in the drum of the tribune of Burlington's Villa at Chiswick and elsewhere in his architecture.

The model for Sevenoaks School and Almshouses is Palladio's Villa Emo, which Burlington may well have seen on his way to the Villa Maser, where he first encountered Palladio's drawings of Roman architecture. The Villa Emo, illustrated in Palladio's treatise,[18] is in the verdant farm country of the Veneto and functioned as a country house and a working farm. All the ingredients for a school and almshouses were at hand in the morphology of the Villa Emo. The owner's residence stands in the centre, and to either side are arcaded wings containing cellars, stables, granaries, and dovecotes camouflaged by the arcades. (Fig. 22) All Burlington did was transform the house into a school and then exchange the farm buildings behind the arcades for almshouses.

We do not know why the design was rejected. Certainly, the £2,500 the school corporation received for the sale of its City property would have been more than enough to erect Burlington's school and almshouses. Perhaps his building complex was considered too ambitious or too large. But even though his design was rejected, the school and almshouses complex that was eventually built reflects Burlington's design in its massing and in some of its architectural detailing.

The Chichester Council House Design

Formed well within the precincts of its Roman walls and divided into four quarters by the two main streets crossing at its center, Chichester, by the beginning of the eighteenth century, was in a state of decay and dilapidation. Reminiscing about the city as it was during his youth, James Spershott (1710-1789) recalled that it had "a very mean appearance."[19] Buildings were, in general, low and very old, their fronts framed with timber that lay bare to the weather. Even in the main streets, few of the houses had solid brick fronts, and the walls encircling the city were broken and in a ragged state.[20] According to Spershott, the process of renovation began about 1724 and continued throughout the eighteenth century and into the nineteenth. In 1731, the old Market House and the old Council House were demolished and a

23
Charles Lennox, 2nd Duke of Richmond, c.1740. Engraved by John Faber after John Vanderbank

new Council House erected with proceeds from a subscription.[21]

By 1730, Burlington was asked by his friend and fellow peer Charles Lennox, the 2nd Duke of Richmond (1701-1750), who, according to Vertue, was "the greatest promoter" of a new council house, to present his design to the Chichester corporation.[22] (Fig. 23) The location of the new council house, which was to replace the old timber-frame structure, was to be on North Street, a major thoroughfare through the heart of the city's administrative centre. The surviving documentation about Burlington's designs is two sets of designs by Flitcroft and correspondence between Burlington and the Duke of Richmond. We do not know why two sets of designs were required, but the sequence of their execution and presentation to the Chichester Corporation can be proved.

By the time of the Chichester Council House, Burlington had worked out a typology for public and quasi-public buildings accommodating large numbers of people. The typology of the arcaded structure derives from his study of Palladio's reconstructions of the Roman baths, a study, it should be noted, undertaken with a critical eye that took the lessons of the baths a step farther and cleansed them of their engaged columns. The result is an astylar arcaded building whose architectural detailing is reduced to its bare essentials and whose rhythms are defined by voids of arcades and windows and the solids of unadorned wall surfaces.

Burlington's first proposal was a long, narrow, arcaded council house, measuring 16' x 86'. The ground floor is an open arcade of three bays on the front elevation and twelve on the side elevations. The first floor is also arcaded, presumably with fenestration intended in the arcade openings and thermal windows above, providing additional light to the interior. (Figs. 24 & 25) The first floor was probably to serve as the council chambers wherein the major deliberations of the Corporation occurred. In the absence of a floor plan, we do not know whether the first floor was one large chamber or was divided into a series of rooms. The design, though rejected, appears to have had an impact on the Corporation and its architect, Roger Morris, in that his council house, erected in 1732, like Burlington's, has an open arcade on the

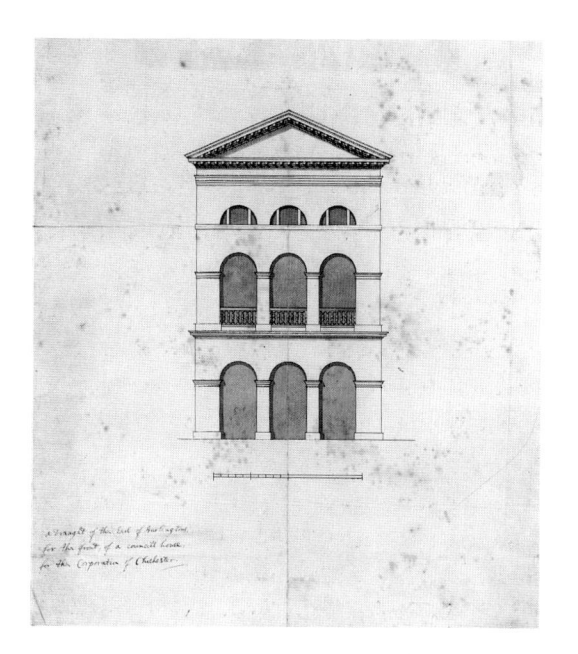

24
Front elevation of the First Design for the Chichester Council House, 1730, Lord Burlington

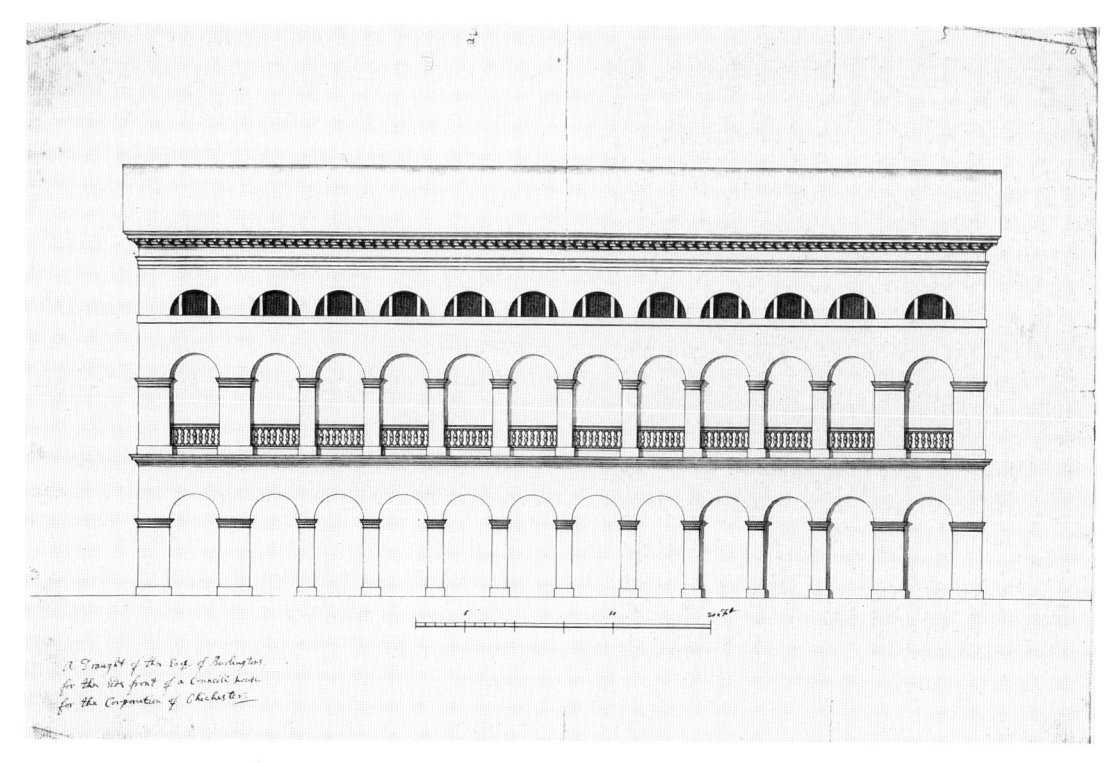

25
Side elevation of the First Design for the Chichester Council House, 1730, Lord Burlington

26
Chichester Council House, Roger Morris

ground floor. (Fig. 26)

The first council house design was rejected either by the Duke of Richmond in his capacity as sponsor and adviser to Burlington or by the Chichester Corporation. Although the circumstances of its rejection are not known, the uncompromising nature of such an arcaded building, its austere appearance, and its possible rendering in white stucco over brick, in contrast to the old timber-frame and new brick buildings of the city would make it a difficult design for a provincial corporation to accept. Furthermore, the second design was much smaller than the first, whose large size may also have been a factor in its rejection. We are fortunate to have an elevation of the second council house design as well as floor plans for it.[23] The central three bays of the front elevation are a replication of the front elevation of the first design, but with the addition of two-storey end bays. The plans of both floors are virtually identical except for the vestibule, where citizens could gather and talk before entering the main body of the council house. Beyond the vestibule is a large rectangular room terminating in an apse defined by a series of six niches. To either side are square rooms, one serving as a city office and one containing a spiral staircase to the first floor. (Fig. 27)

Flitcroft's floor plans provide a rare opportunity to speculate about the character of the interiors of the second council house design. In all likelihood, the apse would have had a coffered half-dome, in the manner of a Roman temple and similar to the half-domes over the apses of the central room of the Gallery in the Villa at Chiswick. (Fig. 28) Burlington was particularly fond of the semicircular shape as a terminus to a room and as expressed in the niches that proliferate throughout his architecture. In San Giorgio Maggiore, he had been drawn to the semi-circular end wall of the choir behind the high altar. Of the choir, he wrote, "[B]ehind the great altar, there is an open intercolumn:^on which discovers the choire, it ends in a semicircle and is one of the most beautifull buildings in the world." [24]

The sense of confinement, then release, that Burlington describes in this annotation is probably the same phenomenon intended for the ground-floor interior of the council house. One would have been led from the vestibule through a narrow entrance into the main chamber and down to the apse at the end of the room. There would have been a dais inserted in the apse and a table and chairs for the Corporation's meetings. Full-length statues of national and city dignitaries would have graced the six niches defining the apse. Presiding over the apse would have been a coffered half-dome painted white, with its salient architectural detailing highlighted in gold leaf. (Fig. 27).

The first floor has virtually the same floor plan as its counterpart below, but

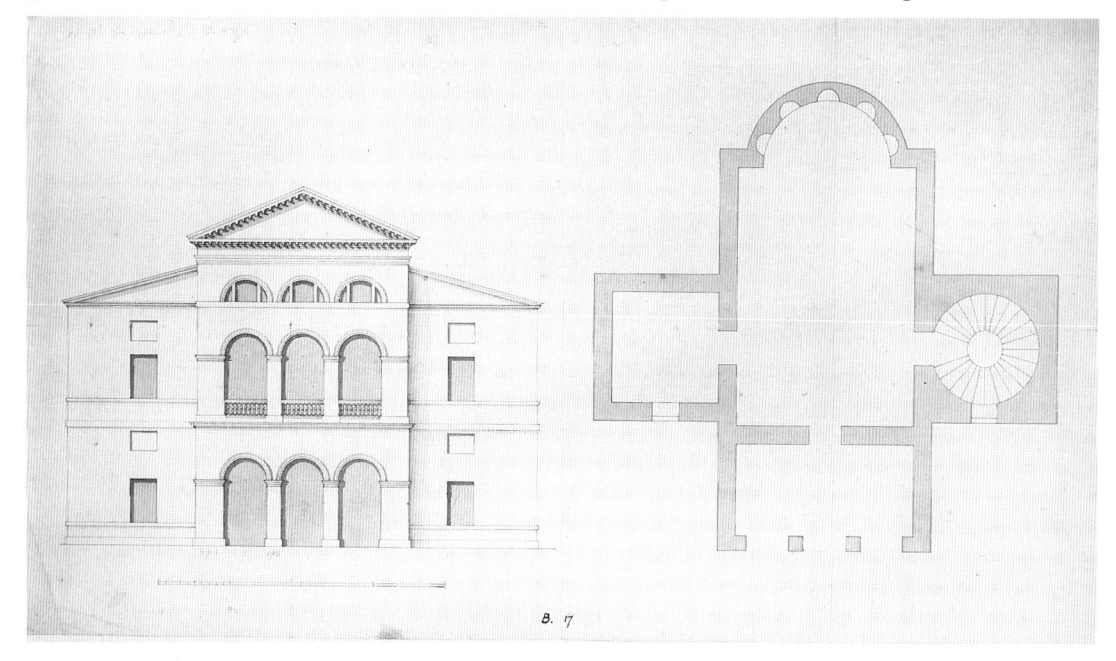

27
Ground-floor plan and elevation of the Second Design for the Chichester Council House, Lord Burlington, 1730

with one significant difference: the chamber is designed to be a double-cube room, twice as long as it is wide, with a ceiling 21' in height (42' x 21' x 21'). The double-cube room is one of seven room sizes recommended by Palladio in his treatise[25] and was favored by Jones in the Banqueting House and by John Webb in the single- and double-cube rooms at Wilton House.

28
The central room of the gallery in the Villa at Chiswick

Like its companion on the ground floor, the first-floor chamber probably would have had an equivalent sense of grandeur and magnificence and would have served as a meeting place for Corporation business and other council affairs. This chamber may have functioned also as an assembly room. This double-cube room would have been the ideal place for assemblies and entertainments, with its domed space at one end and, at the other, a view through arcaded windows of North Street, one of the main thoroughfares of the city. (Fig. 29)

Why was Burlington's second and much smaller design rejected? The answer to this question is to be found in three letters between Burlington and the Duke of Richmond, from a much larger correspondence that has not survived. On 22 June 1730, Richmond wrote to Burlington asking

> if it is not inconvenient to your Lordship, I wish the plan for the council house might be finish'd & left at my house in Whitehall on Saturday next; for you know the season is very far advanc'd, which makes them very impatient, at Chichester, to begin.[26]

Seven days later, Richmond wrote again to Burlington stating that

I must once more beg you to send the plan for the Town house, as soon as possible for the subscription is full, & I am oblig'd to sett out on Fryday next, early in the morning for Chichester, where I dare not go without a plan so I must entreat you, my Dear Lord, to send it to me to my house in Whitehall on Thursday next at farthest, else it will be of no service to me.[27]

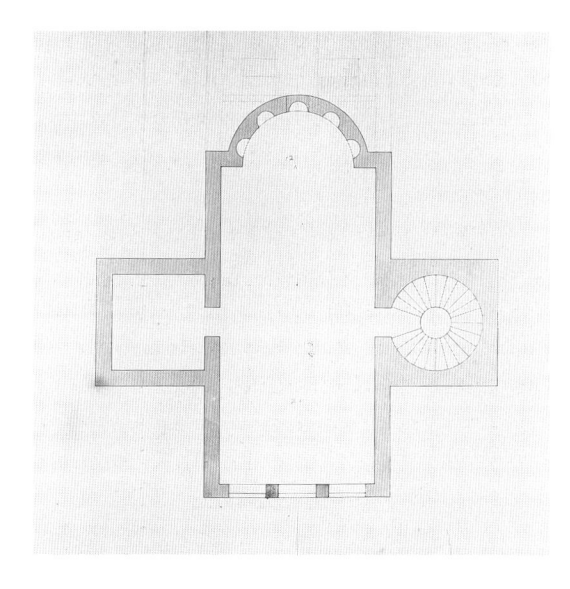

As these two letters suggest, Burlington may well have failed to submit his design at the designated time, and, impatient to proceed, the Chichester Corporation turned to Roger Morris, who had a design immediately at hand.

The Hospital Design

Hospitals proliferated at the beginning of the eighteenth century. After the Reformation, hospitals steadily became secular institutions funded by the Crown and by private donations. By the eighteenth century, they were maintained by charitable trusts funded through subscriptions, wealthy benefactors, or by boards of governors who managed investments and raised capital for building projects. More than anywhere else in England, London urgently needed hospitals to minister not just to the ill and infirm, but to the poor and elderly, and new hospitals abounded there. St. Thomas in Southwark, for example, originally a religious institution and after the Reformation supported by the Crown, was rebuilt on its original site in ca.1701-06 by subscription and the generosity of the City businessman, Robert Clayton. Guy's Hospital was named after the philanthropist and successful printer and bookseller Thomas Guy, who gave £20,000 for a new wing in 1721. There is also the innovative design by James Gibbs for St. Bartholomew's Hospital near

29
First-floor plan of the Second Design for the Chichester Council House, Lord Burlington, 1730

30
Plan for a Hospital, Lord Burlington

Smithfield, composed of four detached rectangular blocks forming a quadrangle and erected over a thirty-eight year period from 1730 to 1768.[28]

The little we know about Burlington's hospital design comes from three drawings that have not as yet led to the identification of the hospital or to the history of its design. However, these drawings do tell us something about Burlington's design procedure. Two of them are by Burlington, the ground plan and elemental line drawing of a side elevation. (Figs. 30 & 31) The third drawing is a finished version of Burlington's ground-floor plan. (Fig. 32) In most instances, Flitcroft, Burlington's chief draughtsman, would have been responsible for finished drawings incorporating Burlington's additions and corrections. In this instance, however, the draughtsman was probably Isaac Ware (d.1766), who, by the early 1730s, had been admitted to Burlington's circle and had access to his drawings collection.[29]

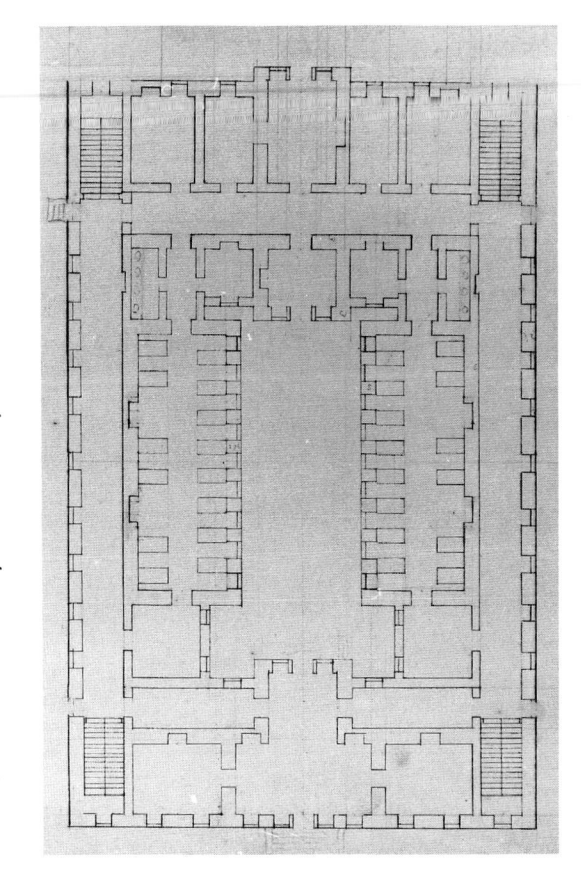

The hospital of Burlington's design is a large, ambitious one, measuring 94' x 189', and has two-storey towers at

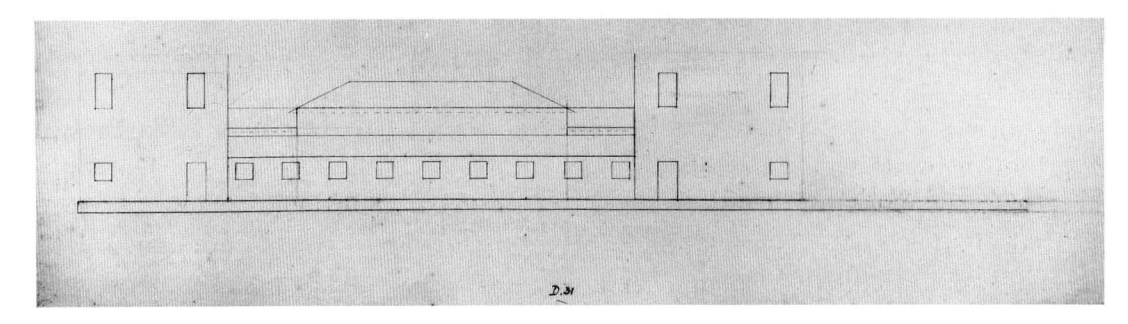

31
Side Elevation of a Hospital, Lord Burlington

40

the corners looking down on a single-storey ground floor. The ground floor is a simple one with an emphasis on easy access and circulation, as well as provision for an abundance of light and air to circulate through the wards. At the heart of the ground floor are two wards, one for male and the other for female patients. Each ward accommodates fourteen beds, two fireplaces, and nine windows looking out onto a courtyard. Long external halls flank the wards and provide circulation around the floor. The rooms on the front and rear of the wards were probably reserved for nurses, doctors, and medical needs such as a scullery and a washroom. The rooms on the front facade and those in the towers probably were meant for administration. (Fig. 32)

It is unfortunate that we do not know the hospital for which Burlington's design was intended. He was a governor of St. Bartholomew's Hospital and could well have learned a great deal about hospital design from Gibbs's drawings and presentation to the board. Perhaps Burlington's hospital design could represent a preliminary study for St. George's Hospital, which resulted from the conversion, from 1733 onward, of Lansborough House at Hyde Park Corner. Isaac Ware was chosen as the architect in competition with Thomas Archer, Gibbs, and others. Burlington was also associated with St. George's Hospital as a subscriber, along with his mother, the Dowager Countess of Burlington.[30] Since Ware and Burlington were colleagues, it is possible that Ware asked Burlington's

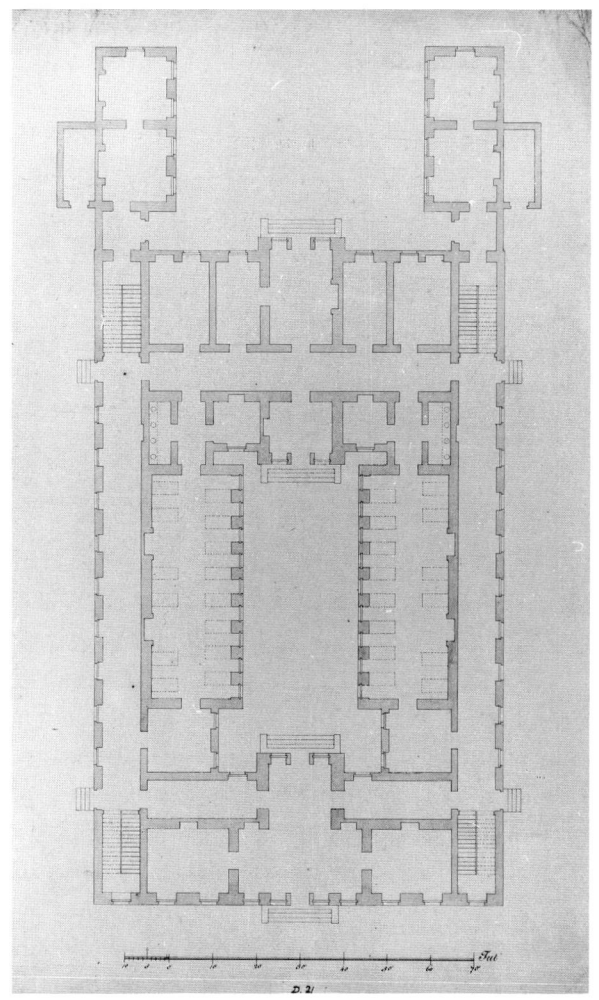

32
Plan for a Hospital, Lord Burlington

41

33
Engraving of St George's Hospital, 1733, Isaac Ware

advice about a suitable hospital design. Burlington responded with a ground plan and side elevation that Ware took one step further, and executed a finished drawing of Burlington's ground-floor plan. (Figs. 32 & 33)

The York Assembly Rooms

The York Assembly Rooms, Burlington's last institutional commission, best exemplify, along with his Villa at Chiswick, his architectural methodology and ideals. Unlike the Westminster Dormitory, tucked away within the precincts of Westminster Abbey and available only to young male students of means, the York Assembly Rooms are located within the Roman and medieval walls of the city in its northwestern section, only a short walk from the York Minster, the city's most important architectural monument. The York Assembly Rooms constitute Burlington's most public building, available to all who subscribed and whose membership included a wide cross-section of the citizens of Yorkshire from the merchants, doctors, and lawyers of the city to the landed gentry and aristocracy of the county. We are fortunate to have an abundance of documentation about the assembly rooms. Their building history and Burlington's involvement with them can be followed in the York Assembly Rooms Minute and Account Books and in a series of drawings. A large site plan has survived and as have four drawings, three of which are probably by Flitcroft and were intended to be engraved. The fourth, a sheet of drawings of the side elevations of the assembly rooms, may have been drawn by Daniel Garrett.

Burlington's assembly rooms were in the forefront of a new building type, created in response to a growing urban culture that required a place in town where the town and country folk could gather for fancy-dress balls, dancing, concerts, entertainment, and private parties. During the first decade of the century, only a very few assembly rooms were erected; rather, entertainment and meetings were held in any available and suitable space large enough to accommodate the needs of the assembled group. Some assemblies met in private homes or in houses that had ceased to function as residences, and others met in rooms of public buildings.

Such was the case in York, where assemblies were held in the Jacobean mansion of Sir Arthur Ingram, located nearby the Minster. During construction of the York Assembly Rooms, the directors met in Carr's Coffee House. Beginning in the 1720s and continuing for the next fifty years or so, assembly rooms were built throughout the country, in popular resorts such as Bath and Tunbridge Wells, in major county centres such as Norwich and York, and in small towns, as well.[31] In the case of the York Assembly Rooms, the directors desired a place where the citizens of York and the gentry and aristocracy of the county could meet, especially during August, when country-house owners were in residence for the assizes and race week at Knaresborough.

Burlington was not the first architect chosen by the directors of the assembly rooms; that honour went to William Wakefield (d.1730), a local Yorkshire resident, gentleman, and amateur architect. Of Wakefield, Sir Thomas Robinson wrote that "had he lived he would have made plans for the York Assembly Rooms 'full as convenient as' Lord Burlington's, and certainly cheaper, 'tho' perhaps [with] not so many Palladian strokes in 'em."[32] Upon Wakefield's death in 1730, the directors of the assembly rooms turned to Burlington, the most illustrious architect in Yorkshire, who resided on his family estate at Londesborough in the East Riding. By May 1730, Burlington had agreed to design the new assembly rooms, and in a letter of 4 May 1730 the directors set out their requirements. First, they stressed that with regard to the design they would "entirely leave to yor Ldship to do in what manner you shall think proper."[33] Then they proceeded to outline what they required:

> What is wanted is a large Dancing room not less than 90 f^t long, another large Room for Cards and play, another for Coffee and Refreshm^{ts} and a Kitchen or place to make Tea in, with a Retiring place of ye Ladies and some where about ye Entrance, perhaps underground, a place with a Chimney for Footmen.[34]

The directors had raised £3,000 for their new assembly rooms, £800 of which was used to purchase the land.[35] Burlington's opinion was that this sum was inadequate, and he raised an additional £500 from his friends. In response to his generosity, the directors raised £500 more. In June 1732, with the cost of construction rising, the subscribers of the assembly rooms agreed to increase the capital stock for the building fund to £5,000 "to finish the Building, with all Expedition and suitable to the Design."[36] But the amount raised was not enough to keep abreast of Burlington's designs and building requirements. Indeed, he had a chronic history of exceeding his building budgets, overspending for the Westminster Dormitory and all his building projects at Chiswick. Sarah, Duchess of Marlborough, in a letter of 9 July 1732 to her granddaughter, Diana, Duchess of Bedford, captures Burlington's profligate building habits with regard to the York Assembly Rooms:

> I stayed at York some hours longer that I designed, to see the cathedral of the place; and the room that my Lord Burlington is building for an assembly by subscription. £5000 is collected already and they are £2000 in debt. I dare say it won't be finished under £20,000 and consequently that it will never be done. For the subscribers, I hear, are extremely weary of it, which I don't wonder at. For it exceeds all the nonsense and

madness that I ever saw of that kind, and that is saying a great deal.[37]

In his 31 October 1730 letter, Burlington informed the directors that "I have sent by S[r] E. Anderson three Drawings in small of the Building. I shall in a short time send them in large, as also Templers in wood for the mouldings and one of my Clerks to reside, upon y[e] spot."[38] The clerk in question was probably Mr. Travers, "my Ld Burlington's workman from Londesborough."[39] The clerk of the works was probably Daniel Garrett (d.1753), an assistant to Burlington, who had developed an architectural practice of his own in the north of England.[40]

The site the directors purchased was an irregularly shaped rectangular plot of land facing Blake Street and only a short distance from Finkle Street and York Minster. (Fig. 34) For this site, Burlington designed a long, narrow building measuring 93' x 140', with a slight indentation on the south side.[41] (Fig. 35) The floor plan of the assembly rooms resembles a basilican church, with a tripartite division of the interior along a longitudinal axis, and a front elevation that has three seemingly separate units, each with what would appear to be its own entrance. The front elevation of the Assembly Rooms owes its character to Burlington's study of Palladio's reconstructions of the Roman baths, but it is an interpretation far more faithful and thus

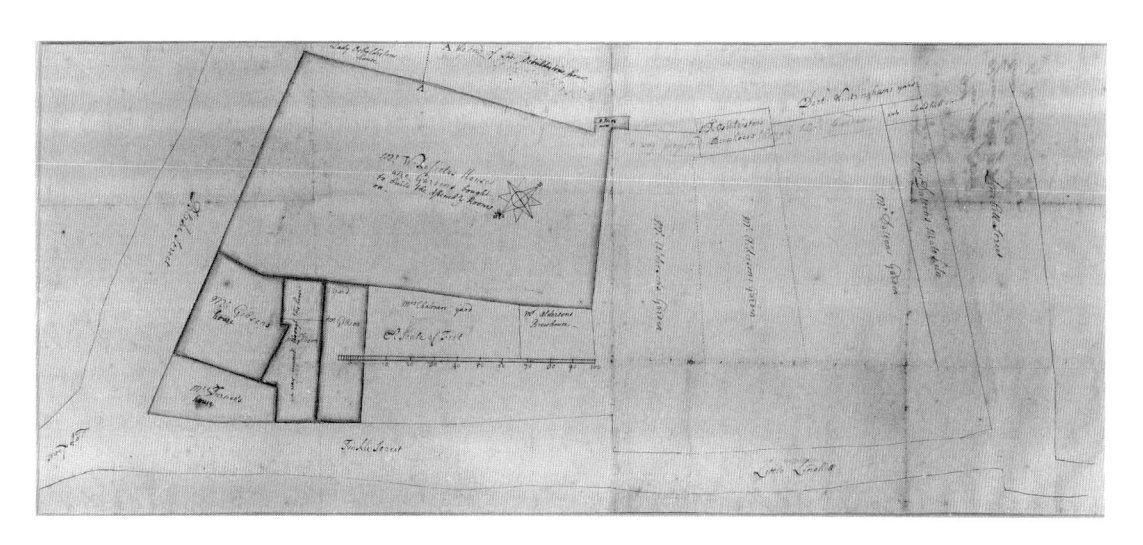

34
Site plan for the York Assembly Rooms, unidentified draughtsman, c.1730

35
Plan of the York
Assembly Rooms, 1730,
Lord Burlington,
Eboracum, 1736

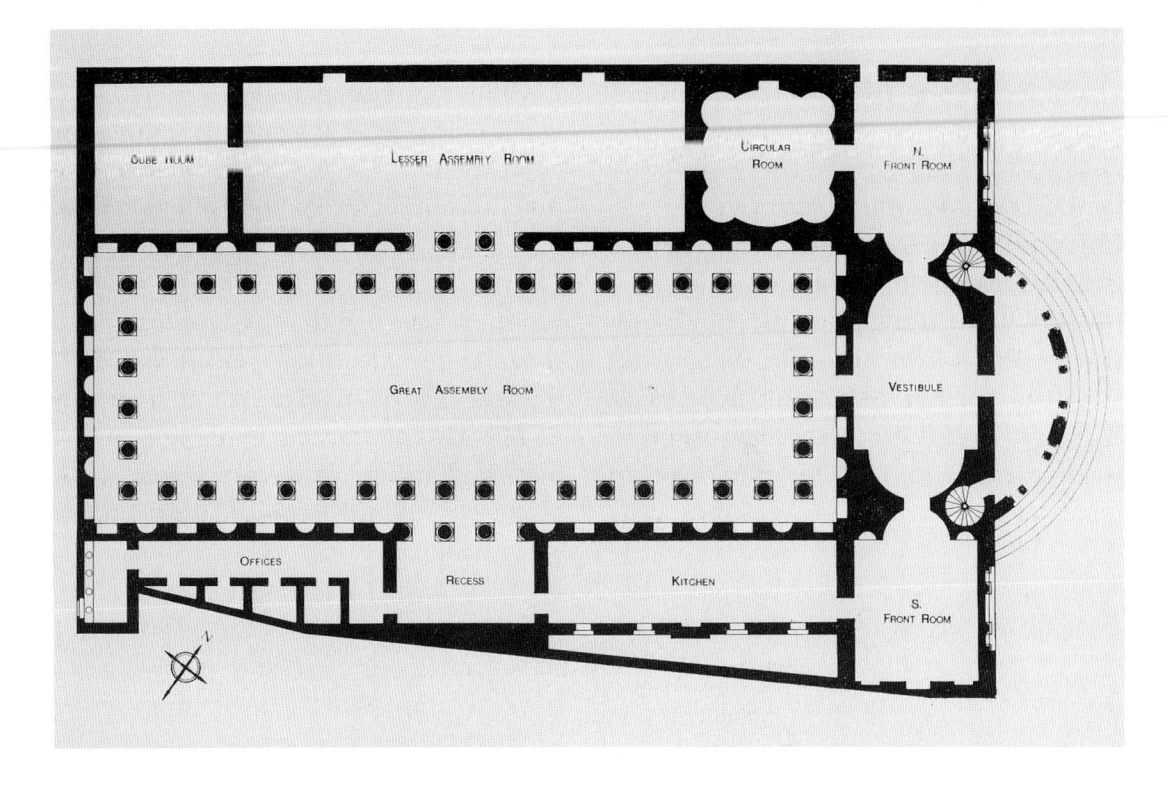

more severe than is found in the Westminster Dormitory or the arcaded design for the Chichester Council House. The five bays of the front elevation consist of tall round-headed openings incorporating Corinthian columnar screens and, above them, unglazed thermal windows. The order of these columns appears to be Palladio's standard Corinthian order in his treatise, the same order as the peripteral colonnade in the Great Assembly Room.[42] The clerestory of the Great Assembly Room rises above the portico and has a balcony with a balustrade, whose balusters, if they could be deciphered in Flitcroft's drawing, would probably be the same ones present on the exterior and interior of the Villa at Chiswick. These balusters are a slightly different version of those in the balcony in the Hall of Jones's Queen's House, Greenwich, that Burlington sent his draughtsman, Samuel Savill, to copy in 1726.[43] The clerestory windows are without frames, which adds to the austere character of the front elevation. A plain hipped roof completes the clerestory. (Fig. 36)

46

Once inside the portico, one saw round-headed niches flanking the entrance to the assembly rooms, and in the corners were circular staircases. One staircase led to the two underground vaults that accommodated the footmen, and the other led to the balcony surrounding the clerestory of the Great Assembly Room. This unusual aspect of the assembly rooms, and one that has not received much attention, is in accordance with Palladio's Egyptian Hall, the model for the Great Assembly Room and its clerestory. The balcony provided a magnificent view of the west and central towers of the Minster, a panoramic view of the city, and a glimpse of the festivities in the Great Assembly Room through the clerestory windows. (Figs. 35 & 36) Evidently, the gallery, as it was called, was a popular place, for at the opening of the assembly rooms in August 1732 tickets were sold "for y

36
Front elevation of the York Assembly Rooms, 1730, Lord Burlington

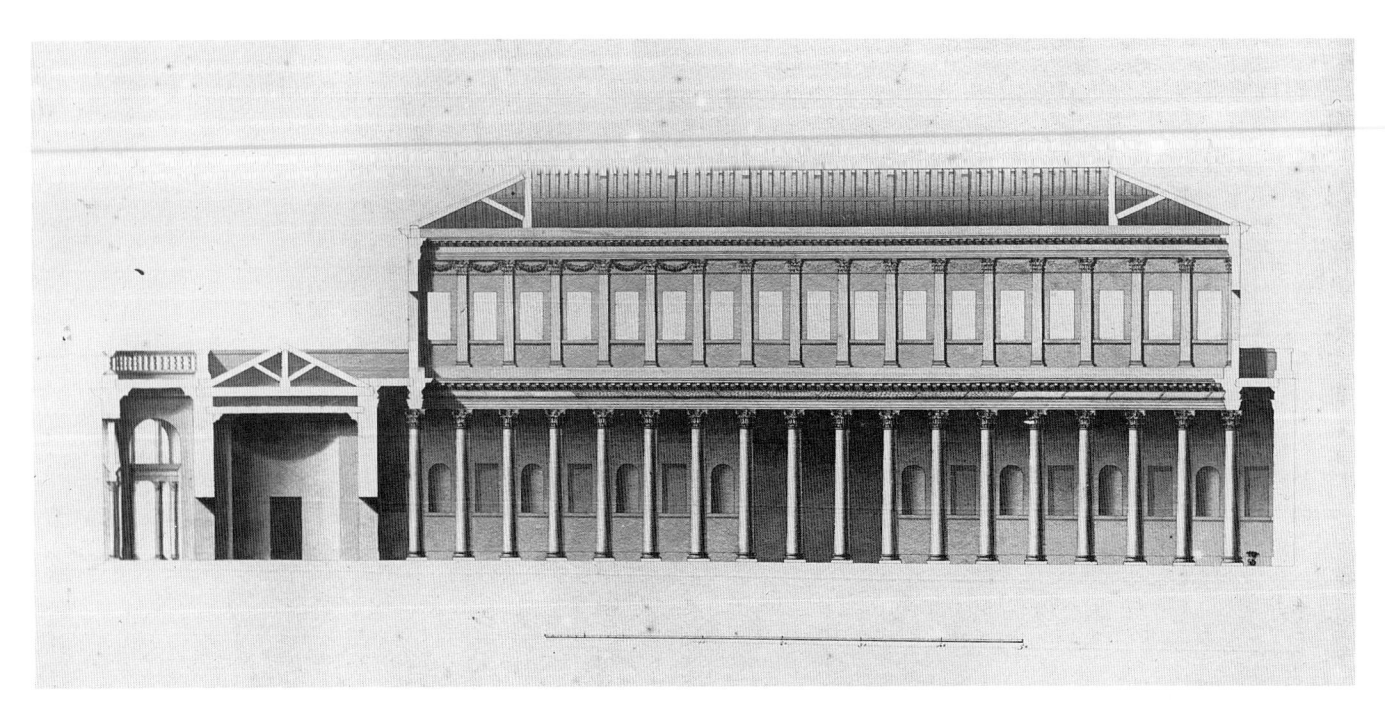

37
Longitudinal section of the York Assembly Rooms, 1730, Lord Burlington

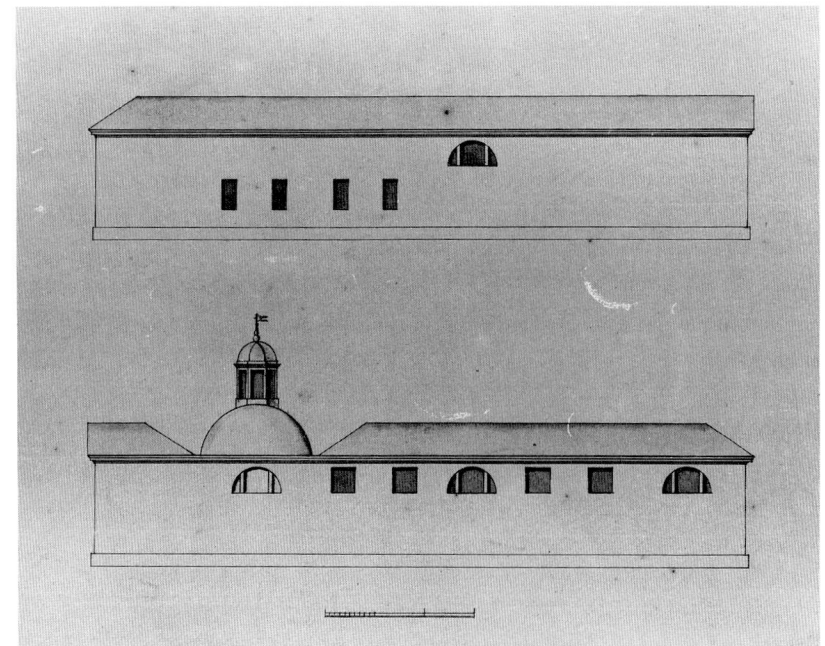

38
Side elevations of the York Assembly Rooms, 1730, Lord Burlington

Liberty of persons going up to the gallery to lookupon y Company."[44] Some, like Sarah, Duchess of Marlborough, were not so sure that the gallery had much merit: "[T]here is a gallery for people to see the dancers, which is so very high that they can see nothing but the top of their heads."[45]

From the portico, one stepped into the vestibule, which, like a narthex of a church, served as a transitional zone between the exterior and interior. The vestibule, reminiscent of the tripartite Gallery in the Villa at Chiswick, consists of a central apsidal room with flanking receiving rooms. They have vaulted apses complementing the apsidal ends of the central room of the vestibule, a fire-place in the opposite wall, and a door leading to a series of rooms flanking the Great Assembly Room. Straight ahead through the vestibule, one entered the glory of Burlington's design, the Great Assembly Room, measuring 40' x 110' and defined by a peripteral colonnade composed of forty-four Corinthian columns. (Fig. 37)

To the right of the Great Assembly Room is a sequence of four rooms of varying shapes and functions. First comes the receiving room, followed by the Circular Room, defined by a series of four round-headed niches that alternate with a fireplace in the outer wall and a pair of doors. This room probably served several functions, as a place for conversation, tea, and other activities involving a small group of people. In addition, it was the antechamber for the Lesser Assembly Room next to it. The Lesser Assembly Room, as its name suggests, accommodated smaller parties and functions not large enough to be held in the Great Assembly Room, particularly during the winter months when activities were reduced in number. This room measured 22' x 66' and had two fireplaces in its outer wall and a two-column screen opening into the Great Assembly Room at its midpoint. Completing the sequence of rooms was the so-called Cube Room, or Card Room. On the other side of the Great Assembly Room were located the service rooms. Beginning with the receiving room to the left of the vestibule, there were a kitchen, a recess with another columnar screen opening into the Great Assembly Room, offices, and another, smaller kitchen or scullery area. (Fig. 35) The fenestration for the side elevations consisted of some of Burlington's favorite window shapes: on the north elevation a series of alternating thermal and square windows, and on the south another thermal window and four double-square windows.[46] (Fig. 38)

Demolition of the old buildings on the site began, and on Monday, 1 March 1731, the foundation stone of the assembly rooms was laid.[47] By late July 1732, the assembly rooms, while nearing completion, still were not ready for use. As Sarah, Duchess of Marlborough, explained in her letter of 26 July 1732, "I was told yesterday that my Lord Burlington comes down to the York races and brings Italians and a great concert of music, which is to be heard in the room which he is building and which is not far enough advanced to have dancing in it."[48] Anxious to open their new assembly rooms for race week in mid-August 1732, the directors decided at their 4 August meeting to convene every day during the second week of August "for the better and more effective furthering of the Work."[49] With minor details yet to be completed, the York Assembly Rooms opened in time for race week. In a letter of 18 August 1732, the directors thanked Burlington for his design as well as for his financial support and asked what remained to be done.[50]

Because no well-defined building tradition for assembly rooms existed to inform and shape Burlington's ideas, he was free to rely upon his own architectural concepts. The genesis of his design for the York Assembly Rooms probably began in Venice in the nave of San Giorgio Maggiore. There, Burlington recorded a comment about the pilaster in one of the nave corners:

> Palladio at the entrance of the church of San Giorgio has placed in the corner, a single pilaster, which stands angular, and fronts on each side. I never saw it any where practiced before, but it has a very good effect, and hinders that confusion which coupled pilasters frequently occasion in angles.[51]

In this annotation, Burlington is concerned with a problem that has plagued classical architecture since the Romans, namely, how to combine the column with the wall in an architecture that is essentially mural in nature. In a building in which the wall is lined with engaged columns, the corner becomes a major problem. A wall defined by engaged columns makes perfectly good sense until one comes to the corner, where it is difficult to place an engaged column without causing "confusion," as Burlington commented in his annotation. The solution he admired in the nave corner of San Giorgio was to insert a pilaster at a right angle into the corner. Thus, all one sees is the sharp right angle of the pilaster as it seemingly emerges from the corner, and not the flat sides of a pilaster folded into it. (Fig. 39) The implication of this annotation and the attitude of clarity and unity it embodies, qualities that characterise Burlington's architecture, are to be found in the Great Assembly Room in York.

The Great Assembly Room is a peripteral hall whose unique character probably is the result of Burlington's observation about the right-angle pilaster in a corner of the nave of San Giorgio, in conjunction with his critical assessment of the interior of Jones's Banqueting House. Since Burlington always based his designs on a classical precedent, either a drawing, a text, or an extant building, it was logical for him to turn to Jones's Banqueting House. The Banqueting House functioned in a fashion similar to the way in which the Great Assembly Room functioned, as a place for royal masques and, later, when Rubens' painting cycle glorifying James I was installed in the ceiling, as a reception hall. The interior of the Banqueting House consists of two storeys and is divided by a cantilevered gallery held aloft by Corinthian consoles. A series of semi-engaged Ionic columns lines the walls of the lower section, with quarter-engaged columns in the corners. Above, in the upper section, Corinthian pilasters line the walls, with folded pilasters in the corners. (Fig. 40) Despite the classical character of the Banqueting House interior, the presence of quarter-engaged columns in the corners of the lower section and folded pilasters in the corners of the upper section creates "confusion which coupled pilasters [or columns] frequently occasion in angles," which Burlington probably found objectionable. In order to avoid

39
Corner in the nave of San Giorgio Maggiore, Venice

40
The interior of the Banqueting House, Inigo Jones

this "confusion" and create a sense of clarity and unity, traits he admired in the nave corner of San Giorgio, Burlington turned to Palladio and his reconstruction of two Roman building types.

For the general morphology of the Great Assembly Room, Burlington selected Palladio's reconstruction of an Egyptian hall, which, according to him, served as a place for festivals and entertainment.[52] The ground floor of the Great Assembly Room is defined by a peripteral Corinthian colonnade from Palladio's standard Corinthian order, but with the addition to the entablature of a pulvinated bay-leaf frieze, a favourite detail in Burlington's architectural vocabulary and one found in great profusion at the Villa at Chiswick. Following Palladio's example, the walls of the Great Assembly Room are defined with alternating round-headed and square niches, and above is a clerestory. (Figs. 41 & 42) The problem with this choice is that only the six columns on the side of the Egyptian Hall are delineated in the treatise, leaving no indication about the length of the colonnade. As a solution, Burlington selected Palladio's reconstruction of a Roman basilica, with its eighteen columns, for the length of the colonnade in the Great Assembly Room. He was prompted to make this choice because of Palladio's statement that the Egyptian Hall resembles a basilica.[53] In the clerestory, however, Burlington deviated from Palladio's Egyptian Hall in that the half columns alternating with clerestory windows were replaced with composite pilasters so that right-angle pilasters could be used in the corners of the clerestory, thus avoiding the "confusion" in the corners. (Fig.43)

41 The Great Assembly Room, York Assembly Rooms

Despite the aura of Roman propriety and grandeur that the Great Assembly Room radiated, from a practical standpoint the room was a failure. The colonnade ringing the room prevented a full view or, in most cases, even a partial view of the dancers. Furthermore, there were no fireplaces to heat the Great Assembly Room and no alcove above ground for a musicians gallery. A gallery had to be created in the recess opposite the Lesser Assembly Room, and the music had to make its way around the columns and out into the room.[54] Sarah, Duchess of Marlborough, the reigning critic of Burlington's assembly rooms, correctly outlined the functional problems besetting the Great Assembly Room:

> It is 98' long and 36' wide between the pillars, of which there are 44, which stand as close as a row of nine pins. Nobody with a hoop

petticoat can pass through them. Three feet is the breadth behind the pillars on each side, which is of no use but to take from the breadth of the gallery, which is much too narrow for the length. This is a room to play in as well as dance, but the windows are as if 'twere a prison and so high that you can't open them to let in air without high ladders.[55]

42
Reconstruction of Palladio's Egyptian Hall, 1570, *I Quattro Libri Dell'Architettura*

43
The colonnade and clerestory in the Great Assembly Rooms, York Assembly Room

44
Engraving of the Great Assembly Room, York Assembly Rooms, 1759, Charles Lindley

One of Sarah's complaints was answered in 1751. At that time, the seats that Burlington had arrayed along the walls of the Great Assembly Room were brought forward and placed in front of the columns of the colonnade. Of course, this decreased the dancing area, which was small to begin with, and ruined the aesthetics of the room. (Fig. 44)

The Roman allusions and associations that permeate the York Assembly Rooms did not go unnoticed by those who saw the building. It was common knowledge that the Great Assembly Room was modelled on Palladio's Egyptian Hall. By selecting the Egyptian Hall, Burlington was associating the assembly rooms with Palladio and, through him, with classical Rome and Vitruvius. Not only did the choice of this model serve Burlington's architectural ideas, the Great Assembly Room and the rest of the building evoked memories of York's Roman past, celebrated in Drake's 1736 history of the city entitled *Eboracum*, the Roman name for York. Drake characterised the Great Assembly Room as "an antique Egyptian Hall" and its architect as "that truly English Vitruvius." Furthermore, he claimed that the city of York possessed in the Assembly Rooms a structure that "in all probability, the Roman Eboracum could never boast of" and that it excelled Eboracum's praetorian palace, where two Roman emperors resided and died and a third probably was born.[56]

In a letter of 6 June 1735, Burlington told his wife that he was leaving Londesborough the next day to dine in York and discuss "a new building which they have desired me to make a design for."[57] The building in question was an addition to the assembly rooms known as the "Piazza."[58] As the directors explained in a letter to Burlington, they required "a Room for the Servants in Waiting, wch is very much wanting to preserve the Front Rooms of the Assembly free from them, who notwithstanding all our Endeavours crowd in wth their Flambeaus & Torches, & spoil the Stucco Work & Chimney Pieces."[59] By June 1735, the directors had purchased from innkeeper George Gibson three pieces of land lying directly to the north of the Assembly Rooms, with two of the plots facing Blake Street.[60] (Fig. 34) As part of the agreement, Gibson retained the right to build above the ground floor of the new building that Burlington was to design.[61] Buildings on one of the two plots of land were cleared, thus revealing the third parcel of land known as the Passage, which led to a side entrance into the north receiving room of the vestibule. It was upon this narrow strip of land that Burlington built his Piazza. The building Burlington designed was a strictly utilitarian structure measuring approximately 18' x 60', with its front elevation facing Blake Street and its single-bay side elevation facing Finkle Street. The seven-bay, arcaded ground floor functioned as a vaulted passageway for the conveyance of chairs to the side entrance of the assembly rooms. A flight of steps connected the passageway to the assembly rooms, and shops were intended to line the rear portion of the arcaded ground floor, in the manner of an Italian Renaissance piazza. In accordance with the directors' agreement with Gibson, the upper two floors were designated for his own use, as indicated by Burlington's notes on the drawing of the floor plans of the Piazza. The front and single-bay side elevations of the Piazza are typical of Burlington's architecture. On the front elevation are double-square windows sitting on a stringcourse, with square windows above them. The single-bay elevation facing Finkle Street has a pedimented window sitting on a stringcourse and a surface enrichment of a gently projecting line sloping out from the wall and flanking the window as if to outline it. This decorative touch to the pedimented window is a characteristic window treatment found on the front elevation of the Link Building at Chiswick and elsewhere in Burlington's architecture. (Figs. 45 & 46)

By 1735, an arcaded building had become a staple of Burlington's architecture. By applying the term "piazza" to the addition to the assembly rooms, Burlington was emphasising the association with Italy and, more specifically, with Jones's "piazzas" that lined two of

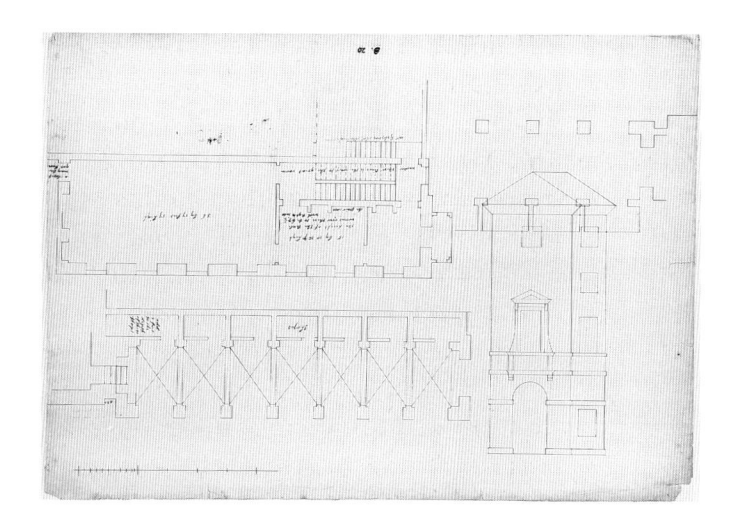

45
Ground- and first-floor plans and elevation of the Piazza, York Assembly Rooms, 1735, Lord Burlington

46
Front elevation of the Piazza, York Assembly Rooms, 1735,

the four sides of Covent Garden. But the Piazza was not built according to Burlington's design. Seven months after the directors had written to thank him for his design and assistance, they ordered that the front "be executed according to this design . . . Except that the Arches be filled up in such a manner as the Directors shall think proper."[62] The ultimate disposition of the arcaded ground floor of the Piazza was quite different from that which Burlington originally had intended. Four of the arches received fenestration, a door was inserted into the fifth, and the last two arches were filled. These alterations to the arcade destroyed the Italianate character of the Piazza and made it far more compatible with the English climate and living style.[63]

The drastic alterations to the Piazza that began during construction only underscore the major problem with it and the assembly rooms. By his unfailing allegiance to classical precedent and, in the case of the Great Assembly Room, to reviving a classical building type, Burlington was able to create a most austere, chaste public building far in advance of Neo-Classicism in Great Britain or on the Continent. With sole control over the design of the assembly rooms and partial control over the Piazza, he was free to follow the dictates of his architectural ideals at the expense of the practical consequences. As a result of this doctrinaire approach, his assembly rooms, whose fame spread throughout the land, did not become the paradigm for other assembly rooms. Although the classical style was preferred, the type of assembly rooms that became popular followed the example of John Wood the Elder's Lindsay Rooms in Bath of 1728. Wood's great assembly room was one large, open hall, with the architectural detailing relegated to the walls and a musicians gallery in an alcove raised above the floor. Where columns were employed, they usually were engaged, or they formed a columnar screen replacing a section of a wall, as in the ballroom of the Bury St. Edmunds assembly rooms.[64]

Chapter 3

The Town Houses

Burlington designed five residences, four of which were intended for London and the fifth for the village of Bishop Burton in the East Riding of Yorkshire. Two of the four London residences, that for General Wade and the other for Lord Mountrath, were erected on land owned by Burlington and located behind the garden of Burlington House. The fourth residence was designed for Lord Pulteney, and the fifth was designed for the 2nd Duke of Richmond and erected in the Privy Garden in Whitehall.

General Wade's Town House

By far the most fascinating of these five residential designs is that for General Wade. The site selected for Wade's town house was behind Burlington House. By 1717, Burlington was deeply in debt and unable to pay tradesmen and creditors. His debt was estimated at about £23,000, a sum virtually equal to his entire annual income of £24,000 in 1721, the year of his marriage to Dorothy Savile.[1] In order to stem his rising debts and to create a new source of income, Burlington opened the five or six acres of land behind Burlington House for housing. Instead of choosing to design a typical London square with rows of houses facing a central garden, Burlington created a series of parallel and crossing streets, all bearing names associated with Burlington and his family: Burlington (now Old Burlington), Boyle (now Vigo), Clifford, and Cork streets. (Fig. 47)

For an architect who concerned himself with every detail of a building, its moulding and its orders, Burlington was surprisingly lax in retaining architectural control of his development. He did, however, retain the right to approve Campbell's facade for the Burlington School for Girls, which was

47
Burlington House and the Burlington Estate development, extract from John Rocque's *Map of London and Westminster*, 1745

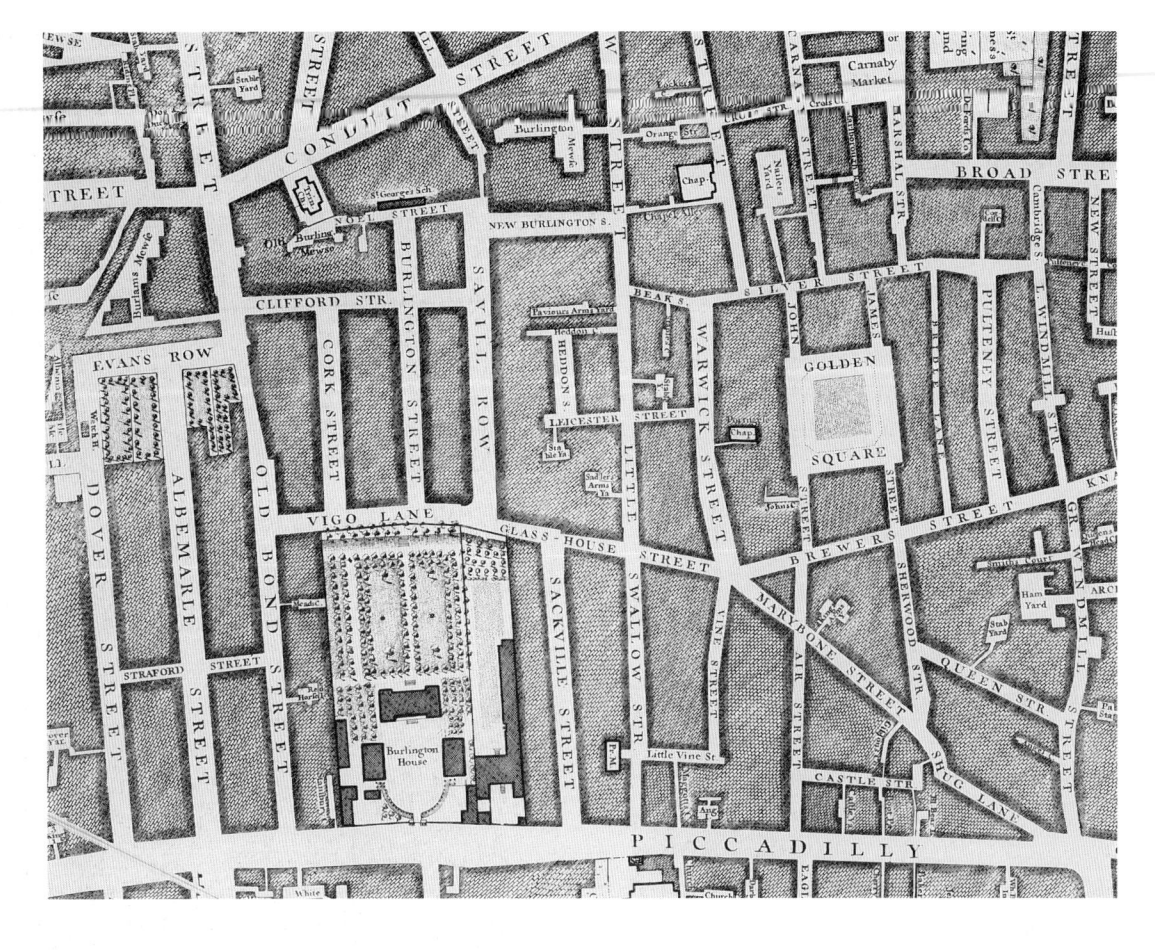

situated on Boyle Street at the spot where Burlington Street terminated and therefore within view from Burlington House.[2] Beyond this, he made no attempt to dictate the architectural character of his development. Nor did he try to coordinate its architecture with that of Burlington House. As a result, a hodgepodge of speculative houses by craftsmen and builders grew up alongside more elegant town houses of the aristocracy, artists, doctors, and lawyers.[3]

George Wade (1673-1748) was a man of sundry talents and interests. Today, he is chiefly known for his military career and as the General Wade who oversaw the construction of roads throughout the Highlands of Scotland so the British government could subdue the Highlanders and their clans.(Fig.48) Wade's other career, which he pursued when not serving in campaigns in Flanders, the Iberian Peninsula, and Scotland, was as a member of Parliament for Bath. Initially, Wade was dispatched to Bath to suppress any Jacobite uprising that might occur as a result of the Jacobite Rebellion of 1715. His introduction to Bath came at a time when the city was just beginning its ascendancy as the premier spa resort in the country. Eventually, he settled in Bath and took up residence at 14 Abbey Church Street next to Bath Abbey, and in time became one of the city's leading citizens and philanthropists. In 1722, he was elected as a Whig to Parliament, a position he would hold for the rest of his life.

Wade's military and political careers have completely overshadowed his activities as a collector and connoisseur with catholic tastes in a variety of the arts. He was a patron of the Italian opera, served on the board of directors of the Royal Academy of Music, and was an avid bibliophile who subscribed to the 1720 edition of Gay's *Poems*[4] and to such architectural texts as volume three of Campbell's *Vitruvius Britannicus* and Kent's 1727 publication of *The Designs of Inigo Jones*.[5] One of his most intriguing acquisitions was an early sixteenth-century Flemish book of hours that at one time had belonged to Henry VII and that Wade, in turn, gave to Burlington.[6] His primary focus, however, was the collecting of paintings. On his death, he had amassed a painting

48
Portrait of General George Wade, attr. to Johan Van Diest

collection that reflected the collecting taste of the day. Like Burlington, Wade favored Italian painting of the Renaissance and the Baroque by such artists as Tintoretto, Raphael, Carracci, Claude, Poussin, and Reni, and a smattering of Northern Baroque paintings by such artists as Rembrandt, Rubens, and Cuyp.[7] He not only collected the Old Masters, but he also commissioned paintings. In 1728, he commissioned the Dutch painter Johan Van Diest to paint portraits of the mayor and aldermen of Bath, which, along with his own portrait, still hang in the Guildhall.[8]

When Wade won election to Parliament in 1722, he required a *pied-à-terre* in London where he could reside while Parliament was in session. If he had not met Burlington before this time, he certainly would have been drawn to him because of Burlington's architectural reputation and because both men shared similar tastes and interests in the arts and in collecting. In 1723, Burlington designed a town house for Wade at 29 Burlington Street. The lot chosen was larger and wider than any of the other lots in the development.[9] Moreover, the town house built on the site was recessed some 13' from the street, its rear garden extending the entire width of the block and terminating at Cork Street.

The first design Burlington proposed was for a site slightly larger than that of 29 Burlington Street. We do not know the reasons for its rejection, but presumably Wade, and possibly Burlington, decided against erecting it. Only two drawings from this first design survive, a plan of the first floor and a front elevation. (Figs. 49 & 50) Since there is little difference between the two floor plans, the objections to the design may have centered on the front elevation. Its cluttered character, with no central focal point and the presence of the Composite order, with alternating

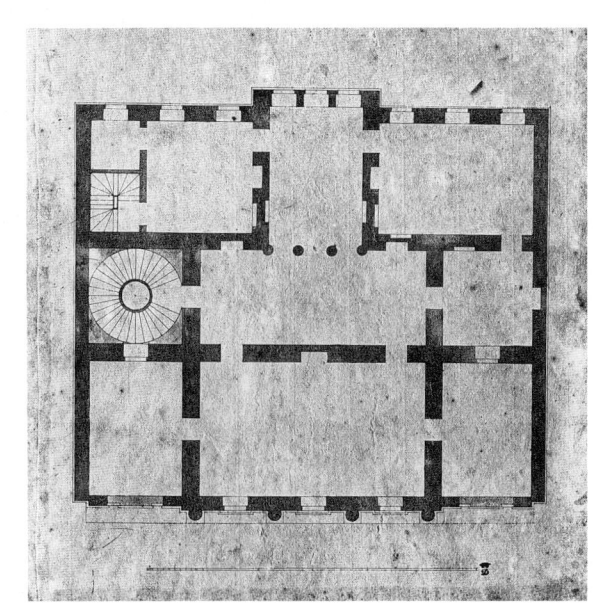

49
First Design of the first floor for General Wade's house, 1723, Lord Burlington

50
Front elevation of the First Design for General Wade's house, 1723, Lord Burlington

51
Front elevation of a *palazzo* design, c. 1550, Andrea Palladio

festoons and decorative heads in the entablature, probably would have made the elevation unsuitable to Wade as well as to Burlington.

The elevation of the second design was far more homogeneous in character and more appropriate to Wade's status as a military officer. But its greatest appeal would have been to Wade's sense of history, associating him with Palladio and the classical tradition. As his model for the elevation, Burlington chose from his drawings collection Palladio's design of a small *palazzo*. The

52
Garden elevation of
General Wade's house,
1723, Lord Burlington

53
Burlington's annotations about Palladio's Palazzo Thiene, in *I Quattro Libri Dell'Architettura*, 1601

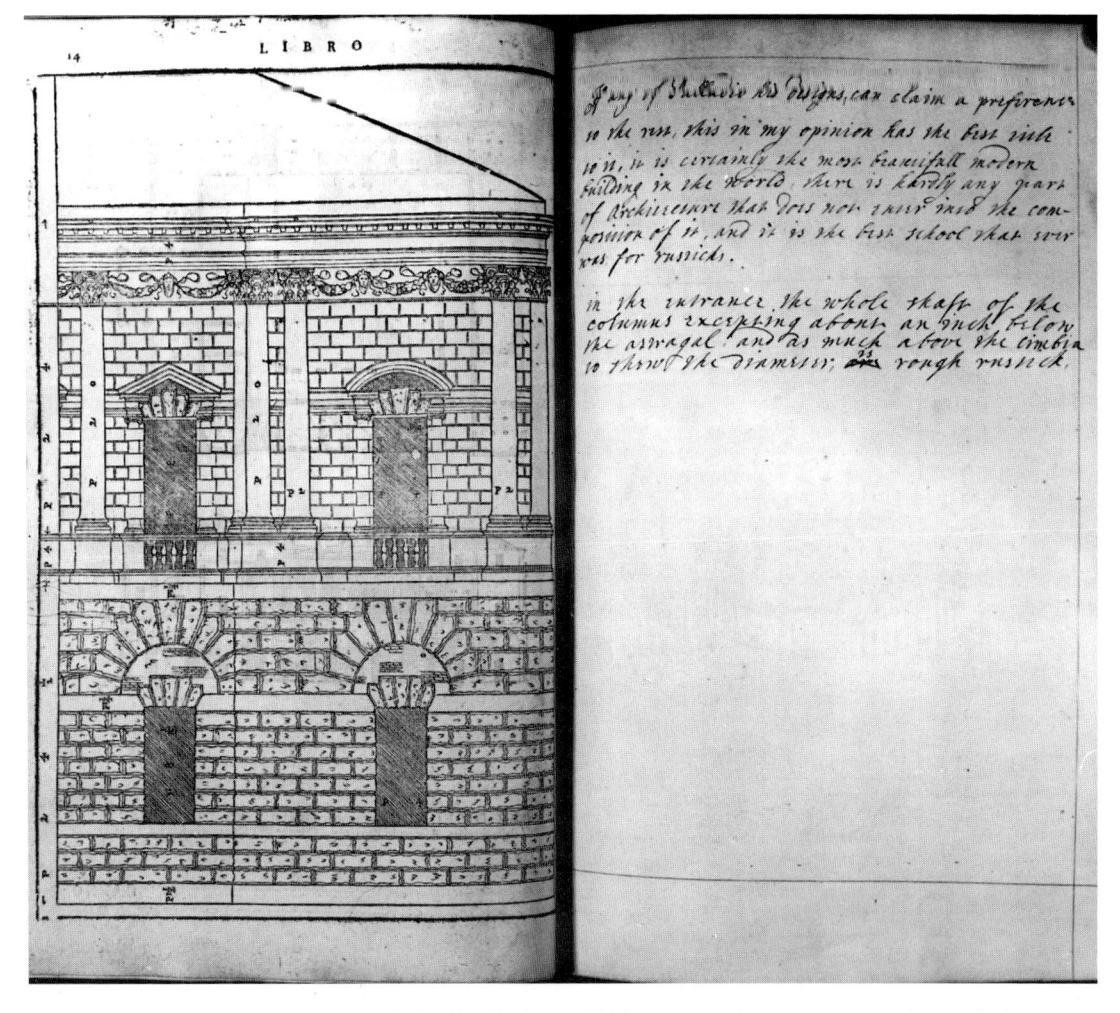

dominant characteristics of Palladio's five-bay, two-storey *palazzo* elevation are the Doric order and the Serliana window on the *piano nobile*. (Fig. 51) Nevertheless, Burlington made three significant changes. The first was to place Palladio's front facade on the garden elevation of Wade's town house. The second was to replace Palladio's ground floor with an arcade. The third change, while not as dramatic as the others, was to cover the piers, voussoirs, and keystones with a strongly textured rustication. The Doric order, with its pilasters and bucranae and paterae in the metopes of the entablature, remained intact and is appropriate for a military man's house, but much of its impact was lost because this elevation faced the garden and not the street, where all could see it. (Figs. 51 & 52)

This highly textured rustication on the ground floor of the garden elevation of Wade's town house was the result of Burlington's study of Palladio's Palazzo Thiene in Vicenza in 1719. His admiration for *bugnato rustico*, a boldly textured rustication that dominates the exterior of the Palazzo Thiene, led him to claim that "it is the best school that ever was for rusticks."[10] (Fig. 53)

Burlington's enthusiastic response was stimulated by the fact that such a boldly textured rustication was rarely found in such abundance on English buildings. Significantly, the first major exploitation of an Italianate rustication was by Inigo Jones, who, like Burlington, was impressed with the rustication on the Palazzo Thiene, which he had studied.[11] Emboldened by the example of Palladio and Jones, Burlington made Italianate rustication a major feature of his architecture. General Wade's town house marked the first time an Italianate rustication had been applied to such a large area of a residence. But at Chiswick Burlington employed an Italianate rustication in an emphatic manner, to the front elevation of the Rustic *Aedicule* and to the entire podium of the Villa.

Until the recent discovery of a drawing of the garden elevation of Wade's town house, we did not know how the facade was executed.[12] Presumably, this drawing represents the garden elevation either during Wade's lifetime or during the ownership of Richard Arundell, a close personal friend of Burlington, who, with his wife, leased the house on Wade's death until the death of Arundell's widow in 1769.[13] This drawing shows that all the salient aspects of Burlington's design were incorporated into the elevation. But two major changes were made. One was the replacement of the ground-floor arcade with two sets of windows and a proper entrance, a change that probably reflects Burlington's final design. The other change was the addition to the roof line of a balustrade. (Figs. 52 & 54) Completing the history of the garden facade of Wade's town house is a photograph of July 1935, just prior to its demolition, showing the addition of an attic storey and the loss of the bucranae and paterae as well as the elimination of the Italianate rustication on the ground floor.[14] (Fig. 55)

54
Garden elevation of General Wade's house, c. 1723-69, unidentified draughtsman

55
Garden elevation of General Wade's house, 1935

56
Design for the garden, 29 Old Burlington Street, after 1769, unidentified draughtsman

Also recently discovered is a drawing of the rear garden and a wall with a gateway facing Cork Street.[15] We know that by 1802 the property contained a large garden,[16] but during Wade's lifetime that area was a courtyard with stables near Cork Street.[17] On the other hand, the tall buttressed wall with quoins covering its corners and a panelled door at its mid-section undoubtedly dates to Wade's ownership. Particularly relevant are the tall piers with rusticated blocks superimposed onto them. The rustication on the blocks is boldly textured and suggests the presence of an Italianate rustication echoing the rustication covering the ground floor of the garden elevation. (Fig. 56)

Very little is known about the interiors of the town house or how they functioned. Originally, Burlington intended eight rooms with coved and vaulted ceilings on the ground floor. (Fig. 57) The ground floor as built, however, was identical to the first floor and consisted of six rooms, a spiral staircase at one side for the servants, and a more elaborate half-turn staircase with landings to either side for Wade and his guests.[18] Presumably, each floor had two 18-foot-square rooms in the corners of the front elevation flanking a hall or antechamber leading into the 20' x 30' saloon on the garden facade. (Fig. 58) Burlington intended a Serliana window on the front elevation to complement the one on the garden elevation, but, judging from a 1935 photograph of the front elevation, it was not built. Excluding the nineteenth-century addition of the semicircular entrance and the attic storey, this photograph

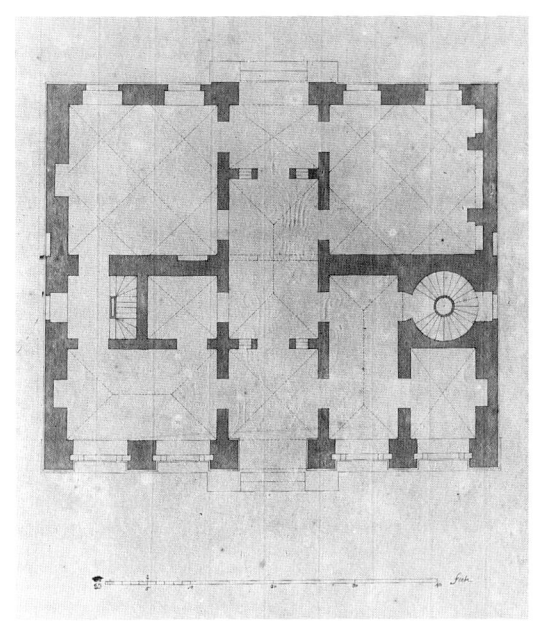

57
Ground-floor plan of the penultimate design for General Wade's house, 1723, Lord Burlington

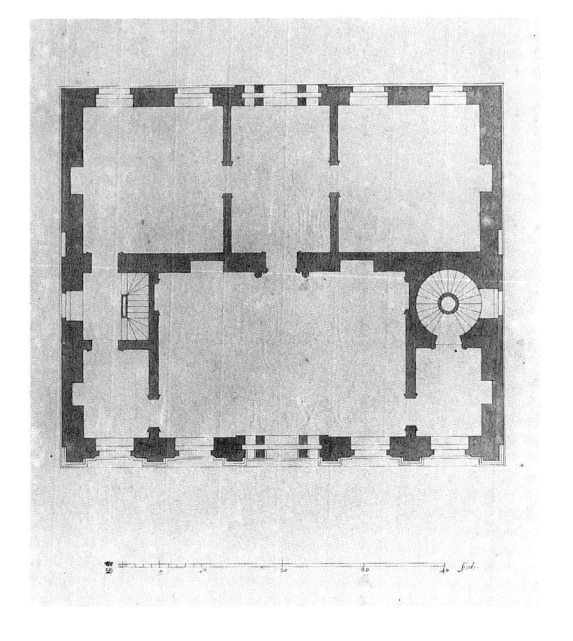

58
First-floor plan of the penultimate design for General Wade's house, 1723, Lord Burlington

shows the elevation as it was during Wade's lifetime: the first two floors with double-square windows, a chamber floor with square windows, and a balustrade to complement the one on the garden elevation. (Fig. 59)

59
Front elevation of General Wade's house, 1935, Lord Burlington

According to Horace Walpole, the only instruction Wade gave to Burlington concerning the town house design was that he provide a place to hang Rubens' large cartoon *The Calydonian Boar Hunt*.[19] The cartoon, which Walpole claimed Wade "had bought in Flanders,"[20] undoubtedly was the prize piece of art in his painting collection and was, indeed, huge, measuring 10'7" x 20'9 1/2".[21] (Fig. 60)

Unfortunately for Wade, there was no wall space large enough to accommodate it, because, according to Walpole, Burlington "found it necessary to have so many correspondent doors, that there was no room at last for the picture; and the Marshall was forced to sell the picture to my father: it is now at Houghton."[22]

General Wade's town house was controversial during its day, both damned and praised. Walpole thought "it is worse contrived on the inside than is conceivable, all to humour the beauty of the front. My Lord Chesterfield said, that to be sure he could not live in it, but intended to take the house over against it to look at it."[23] The self-appointed architectural critic James Ralph praised the town house,

which tho' small, and little taken notice of, is one of the best things among the new buildings: the general design, or plan, is entirely chaste and simple; and yet the execution is pompous and expensive: indeed the whole house is one continued clutter

60
The Calydonian Boar Hunt, engraved by Richard Earlom after Peter Paul Rubens, 1781

of ornament, and yet there is no body can say there is too much, or that he desires to have any part remov'd out of the way: let me add, 'tis the only fabrick in miniature I ever saw, where decorations were perfectly proportion'd to the space they were to fill, and did not by their multiplicity, or some other mistake, incumber the whole[.] [24]

Despite the harsh comments of Walpole and Chesterfield, Ralph's comments elucidate a primary principle of Burlington's architecture. Ralph characterized the town house as "small" and a "fabrick in miniature," but, nevertheless, possessing what Joseph Addison has termed a "Greatness of Manner." [25] As Pope stated in the argument of his epistle to Burlington, "the first great Error . . . is to imagine that Greatness consists in the *Size* and *Dimensions* instead of the *Proportion* and *Harmony* of the whole." [26] Architecture, then, is not merely a matter of possessing the financial resources to build on a vast scale or size; rather, it depends upon the Renaissance concept of scale, which is based on the human figure. By means of what Ralph calls perfectly proportioned decorations, that is, the Doric order

71

and architectural detailing, Wade's town house projects an aura of magnificence and grandeur that belie its diminutive size.

Lord Mountrath's Town House

Burlington, working in association with Colen Campbell, designed a residence for Algernon Coote, the 6th Earl of Mountrath (d.1744), located at 30 Burlington Street next to General Wade's town house. Mountrath, like Wade, was of Irish descent, a member of the British and Irish Parliaments, and served on the Privy Council of Ireland.[27] In all likelihood, Mountrath approached Burlington about the design of a London town house where he could reside during sessions of Parliament. By March 1721, his name appears as one of the tenants in Burlington's development, but, for some inexplicable reason, he decided not to occupy the house and took up residence in St. James's Square.[28] Because of this early change of ownership, which probably occurred during construction, Burlington and Campbell were responsible only for the fabric of the house and the front elevation, but not for the design of the interiors. Michael Newton, the first occupant of the house, probably determined the character of the interiors. However, Campbell may well have been hired as the architect for the interiors, which were famous during their day. A photograph of the walls and ceiling of the staircase shows a decorative treatment similar to what Campbell was doing at Wanstead and Mereworth.

With regard to the front elevation of the town house, Campbell's hand predominates, but Burlington's presence is definitely felt as well. Burlington signed Flitcroft's presentation drawing of the front elevation "for Ld Montrath London," as if to give his imprimatur to the design and to make the point that Mountrath was his friend. (Fig. 61) Campbell's sheet of drawings depicts the penultimate stage of the design. The ground-floor plan was altered to include a much larger and grander staircase, and the shapes of other rooms were altered, too. (Fig. 62) The only difference between Campbell's and Flitcroft's presentation drawings of the front elevation is Burlington's addition of some of his favorite motifs: tall chimney stacks to each side of the hipped roof and rusticated quoins on the corners below the ground-floor stringcourse. (Figs. 61 & 62)

Certainly, the front elevation is not the virtuoso performance that characterises the garden elevation of Wade's town house. Rather, it is very conventional and owes its general form and rather plain character to Campbell. As in Burlington's architecture, architectural detailing is kept to a minimum and relegated to the fenestration and the entrance. The proportions of the fenestration, double- and single-square openings, are also characteristic of Burlington's architecture but can be found in Campbell's architecture as well. The main emphasis is on the aedicular entrance, with smooth-faced blocks superimposed onto the Ionic columns and rusticated voussoirs, and a keystone superimposed onto the pulvinated entablature. This aedicular entrance, minus its rustication, is taken from Jones' entrance illustrated in Kent's *The Designs of Inigo Jones*, which Burlington probably recommended in order to enliven the facade.[29] Such an aedicular entrance, known as a Gibbs surround, can be found throughout Campbell's architecture but appears only once in Burlington's.[30] The central light on the first floor is pure Campbell, a tall round-headed window framed by Ionic

61
Front elevation of Lord Mountrath's house, c.1721, Lord Burlington and Colen Campbell

62
Ground-floor plan and front elevation of Lord Mountrath's house, c.1721, Lord Burlington and Colen Campbell

73

63
Front elevation of Lord Mountrath's house, 1935

columns supporting an architrave. Nowhere in Burlington's architecture would one find the repetition of the same order on two consecutive floors, as occurs in this elevation. The powerful entablature with a pulvinated frieze, not present in either drawing, was probably Burlington's addition and is an allusion to engaged columns or pilasters and thus a metaphor for a temple front. (Figs. 61 & 63)

Burlington may well have lost interest in the design once his friend Mountrath forfeited his tenancy and moved to St. James's Square. At this point, Burlington relinquished control of the design to Campbell but reserved the right to insert details to his liking, such as the addition of rusticated quoins. The elevation of the Mountrath house looks remarkably similar, in all but its roof treatment, to Campbell's residential design for Henry Pelham at 32 Burlington Street.[31]

A Design for William Pulteney's House

We know nothing about the palatial residence that Burlington designed for William Pulteney (1684-1764) other than what we learn from Flitcroft's two sheets of drawings containing the ground- and first-storey floor plans and front elevation. Neither of these two sheets is dated, and the only means of identifying them is Burlington's inscription on the sheet containing the front elevation "for Mr. Pulteney." (Fig. 64) William Pulteney was a staunch Whig, a life-long member of Parliament, and an arch foe of Robert Walpole and his administration.[32] The residence Burlington designed for him was his most ambitious and the largest of all his residential designs, boasting a front elevation far more appropriate in Italy than on a London street. Pulteney was a man who savoured his wealth, and

64
Front elevation of William Pulteney's house, c.1720-27, Lord Burlington

Burlington's design, the front elevation as well as its spacious interiors, reflects Pulteney's wealth and social position.

The facade of the house is extremely Italianate in character but far more open and accessible than any of Palladio's *palazzi*. Indeed, it would seem that this residence had no one prototype or model, Palladian or otherwise. The design for Pulteney's residence is probably an early one and perhaps executed in the first part of the 1720s along with the town houses for Mountrath and Wade but not after 1727, when the floor plans and elevations are illustrated in *The Designs of Inigo Jones*.[33] The decorative, cluttered quality of the facade and the engaged columns are all elements that Burlington eliminated in his mature work at Chiswick and in his institutional buildings, such as the designs for the Chichester Council House and the York Assembly Rooms. However, several

65
First- and second-floor plans of William Pulteney's house, c.1720-27, Lord Burlington

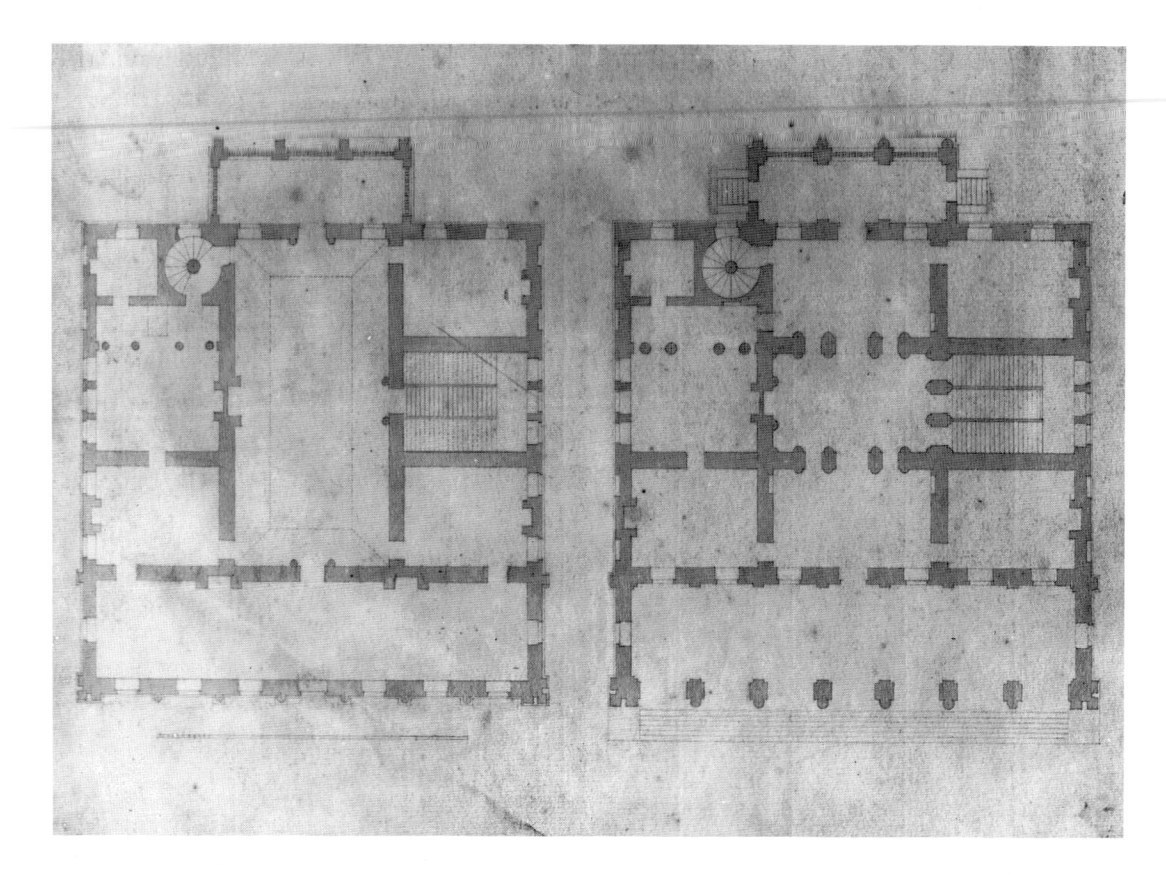

architectural elements of the Pulteney residence became staples of Burlington's architectural vocabulary: the double- and single-square windows, the double-cube room, and the rooms defined by a columnar screen, the one on the first floor being Pulteney's bedroom. (Figs. 64 & 65) We do not know why the house Burlington designed was not erected, but surely the very Italianate, impractical nature of the facade militated against its ever being built. Nor do we know where Pulteney intended to erect the residence Burlington designed for him. It may well have been just to the east of Burlington's development on land that was part of the Pulteney estate and that Pulteney opened for development from 1719 onward.[34]

THE DUKE OF RICHMOND'S HOUSE

The third and last house that Burlington designed and built in London was for the 2nd Duke of Richmond, who had attempted to obtain for Burlington the commission for the Chichester Council House. The site for Richmond's residence was in Whitehall at the southern end of the Privy Garden facing the Thames. In 1710, the 2nd Duke's father, the 1st Duke of Richmond, obtained a lease for this site and built a house on it.[35] At his death, his son obtained a new lease to the property as well as a lease to a slip of land on which he intended to erect a wall for his own privacy.[36] By May 1733, he had demolished his father's house and had begun the process of erecting a new residence designed by Burlington.[37]

The design for the new Richmond House progressed in at least two stages, if not more, from a first design to a second design, and, quite possibly, changes and alterations to the second design that resulted in the residence as built. All the extant drawings, the first set of four drawings and the second set of ten bound drawings, were, in all probability, by Daniel Garrett, who was involved in the construction of the York Assembly Rooms and was probably the site architect for Richmond House.[38]

We do not know much about the first design, because the four surviving line drawings are not very informative. The house was to be 61 1/2 feet in length with seven bays and two storeys and with a broad blank space above the first floor windows, suggesting that an attic storey was intended. (Fig. 66) The three drawings of the ground floor vary only slightly and depict a series of rooms around a central spiral staircase and an unassuming entrance relegated to the far left side of the house, which was probably a servants' entrance with its own staircase. On one of these drawings, above the servants' entrance, is the inscription "Door to the Terrass," referring to the terrace between Richmond House and the Thames, which afforded magnificent views of the river, the City, and St. Paul's Cathedral. The servants' entrance is part of a small addition to what is otherwise a rectangular house plan. (Fig. 67) Its presence suggests that at least part of the new Richmond House probably utilized the foundations of the old

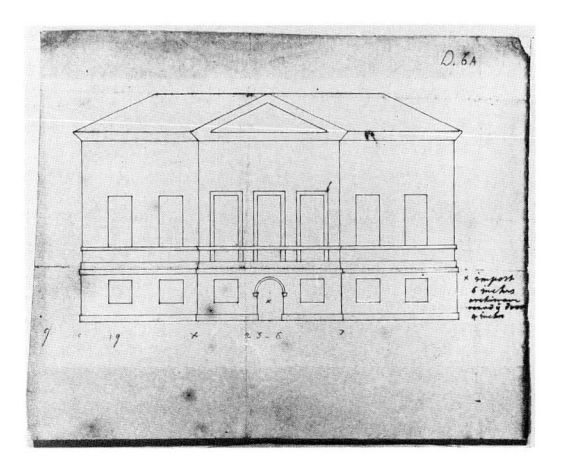

66
Front elevation of the First Design for Richmond House, c.1732, Lord Burlington

Richmond House. Whether this servants' entrance was ever built cannot be ascertained, but it is not accounted for in the drawing of the front elevation. (Fig. 66)

67
Ground-floor plan of the First Design for Richmond House, c.1732, Lord Burlington

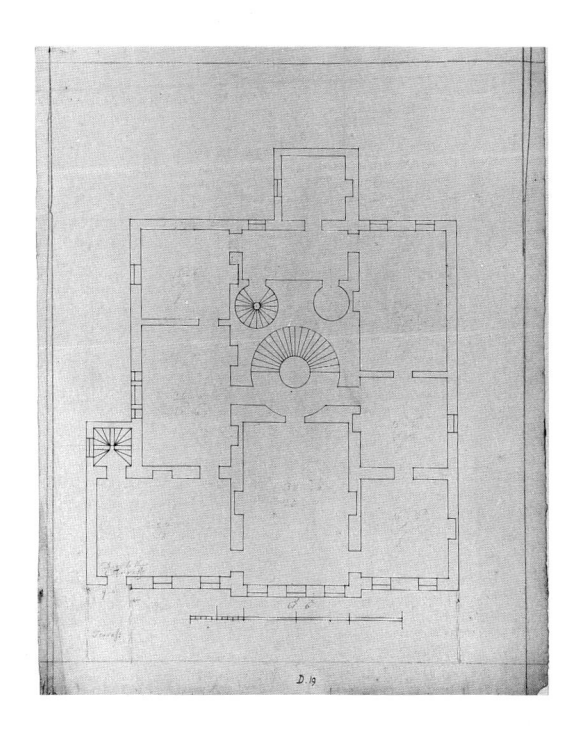

The other set of drawings is a series of ten drawings bound in leather and bearing the inscription "A Plan of His Grace the Duke of Richmond House in White-Hall." Included in the volume are drawings of a front elevation; floor plans for the cellar, principal, and attic floors; the ceilings in the dining room, drawing room, and salon; and plans for a three-storey, detached kitchen. In all probability, the volume represents transitional designs from which would emerge the final design for Richmond House.

The front elevation of the second design, like the other elevation, has seven bays, but unlike its counterpart has an attic storey and measures 39 feet in height to the roof line. This elevation can best be characterized as one of austere simplicity in keeping with Burlington's mature work. The windows are unadorned, and there are no engaged columns or pilasters decorating the facade, only a modillion cornice and a slightly projecting pediment over the central three bays of the facade, a reminder of an order not present on the facade. The only architectural detailing is relegated to the entrance and the central window of the first floor. (Fig. 68) There are marked similarities between this elevation and the front elevation of the Link Building at Chiswick, which connects the Villa to the Jacobean House and the Summer Parlour and which was probably under construction by 1732, the same time as Richmond House was under construction. (Figs. 68 & 69)

The drawing of the principal storey in the second design differs only slightly from that of the first design. Once again, several standard elements of Burlington's architectural vocabulary are present: spiral staircases, a bedroom with a columnar screen, and Serliana windows defining the side elevations, as found on the Villa at Chiswick. This drawing raises the question of the location of the principal storey. Is it, like its companion from the first design, located on the ground floor? This was not an unusual arrangement in eighteenth-century London but certainly at variance with the Palladian practice of having the formal rooms on the first floor.[39] On the other hand, are the dotted lines running across the servants entrance in the far left corner an indication of an intended wall? And is what seems to be the main entrance in the centre of the elevation actually the pedimented window that also acts as a door opening onto the balcony? This same arrangement is found in the central room of the Gallery at Chiswick where the Serliana window doubles as a door opening onto the garden balcony. (Fig. 70) In all probability, the principal storey was located on the first floor, if only for the reason that the room with the columnar screen and a penciled-in bed is probably a bedroom,

68
Front elevation of the Second Design for Richmond House, c.1732, Lord Burlington

69
The Link Building, Chiswick Villa

and bedrooms usually were located on the first floor.

The three-storey kitchen included all the domestic rooms necessary to serve Richmond House. The drawing of the kitchen has four windows on one side, including a Serliana window, and an entrance on the opposite wall, with what would appear to be a side elevation joined to another building. (Fig. 71) Where the kitchen building was located in relation to Richmond House is difficult, if not impossible, to determine. Rocque's 1746 map of London and Westminster shows a small projection on the west side of the stable yard near Richmond House. But Canaletto's view, *Whitehall and the Privy Garden Looking North*, shows no kitchen within the confines of the stable yard.[40]

It is also difficult to determine the actual disposition of the exteriors of Richmond House. All that can be said with any degree of certainty is that they were significantly different from the elevation and floor plans of the second design. Our main sources of information about the exteriors of the house are a 1747 view by Canaletto and a 1749 engraving. Canaletto's view, one of two stunning views commissioned by the 2nd Duke and now at Goodwood, depicts just a portion of the rear, southeastern corner of the house and part of Richmond Terrace facing the Thames. On the rear of the house are an elaborate bay window, which is not part of any of the extant floor plans, and two pyramidal chimney stacks, also not found on any of the drawings.[41] Similar pyramidal chimney stacks are found at the Villa at Chiswick and were inspired by pyramidal chimney stacks atop many of the *palazzi* on the Grand Canal that Burlington would have seen on his two trips to Venice. The honey-

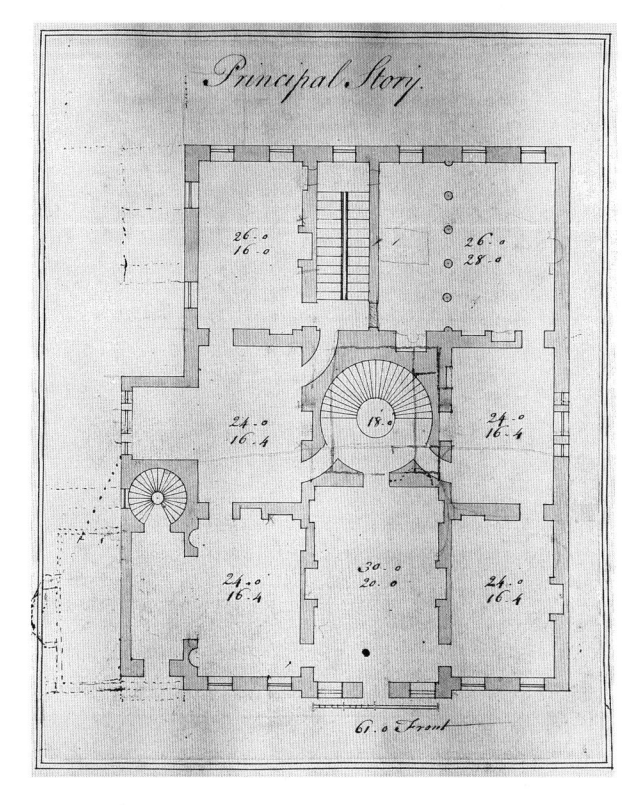

70
Principal-floor plan of Richmond House, c.1732, Lord Burlington

71
Floor plan of the kitchen for Richmond House, c. 1732, Lord Burlington

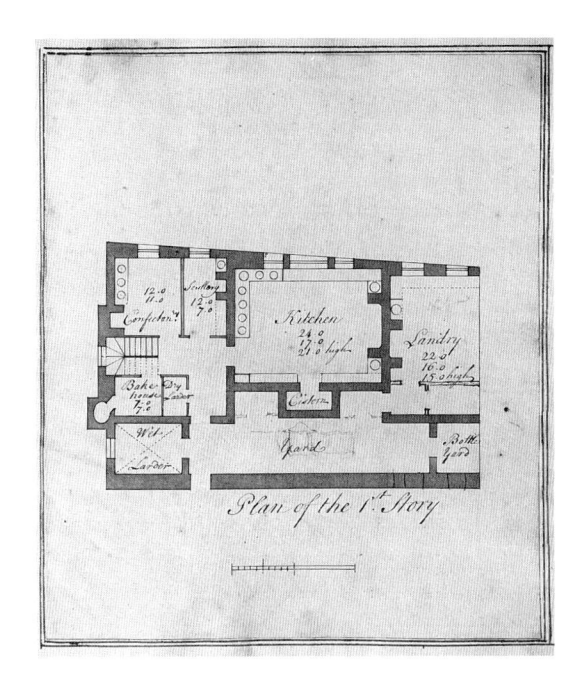

coloured stone covering the house, but not the bay window, is probably Bath stone, which by the 1730s was winning favour in London and was used by Burlington for the Westminster Dormitory.

The 1749 engraving provides the most complete contemporary view of Richmond House. The house forms the background to an elaborate fireworks display that the 2nd Duke gave in celebration of the Peace of Aix-la-Chapelle, ending the War of the Austrian Succession. This celebration was attended by the King and court dignitaries in barges on the Thames.[42] The front elevation of Richmond House is shown facing north toward Charing Cross and is somewhat similar to the elevation of the second design, but without any indication of an entrance or fenestration on the ground floor and with a Serliana window at the corner of the side elevation, a rather odd position for such a window.[43] (Figs. 68 & 72)

We are fortunate, indeed, to have drawings for three of the beamed ceilings in Richmond House, which offer a hint of the sumptuous character of the interiors of the house. The beams are richly decorated with such standard classical motifs as the Greek key pattern, festoons alternating with decorative heads, the Vitruvian scroll, and fully developed cornices. (Figs. 73, 74, & 75) In all probability, oil paintings were inserted into at least the central panel of each of the ceilings. The oil painting *Neptune, Mercury, Zephyrus, and Flora*, attributed to William Kent, may well have been placed in the oval of the ceiling of the drawing room.[44]

Since it is possible to determine the dimensions of each ceiling, the rooms in which they were located can be identified. All these rooms were on the first floor of the house. The salon, with its ceiling measuring 20' x 30', was probably located in the centre of the

72
Engraving of a Fireworks Display on the River Thames, 1749

first floor. To the left was the dining room, with a ceiling measuring 16' x 24'. Adjacent to it was the servants' spiral staircase to provide efficient access to the dining room. The wide entrance leading to the small spiral staircase would seem to be the result of Richmond's request made to Burlington in an undated letter saying,

"[P]ray remember to keep the opening to the bufett in the dining room as wide as possible."[45] The drawing room, its ceiling measuring 16' x 24', was probably located to the right of the salon in the corner. (Fig. 70) The windows of all three of these rooms offered a magnificent view north toward Charing Cross to the City and

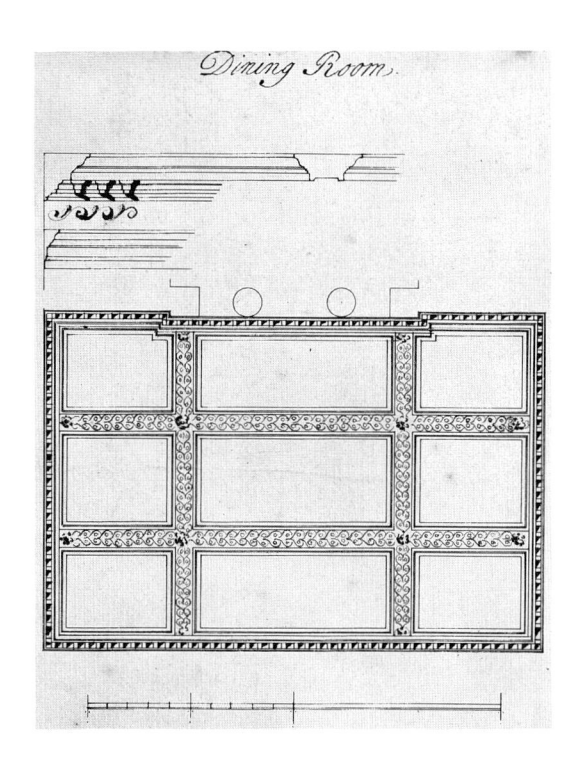

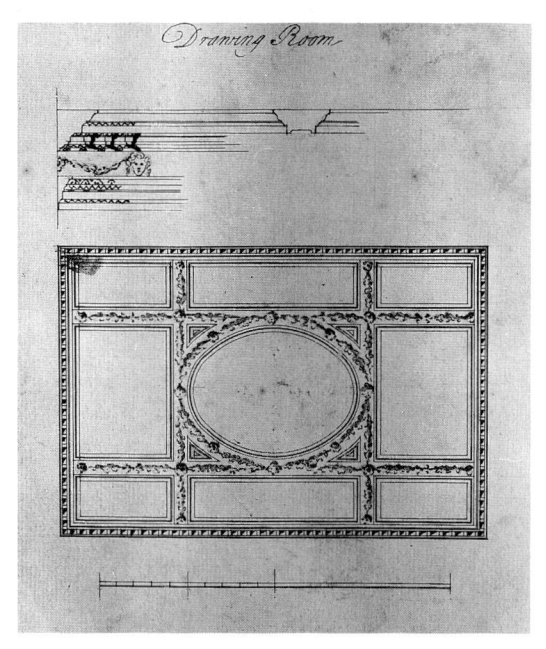

73
Design for the dining-room ceiling of Richmond House, c.1732, Lord Burlington

74
Design for the drawing-room ceiling of Richmond House, c. 1732, Lord Burlington

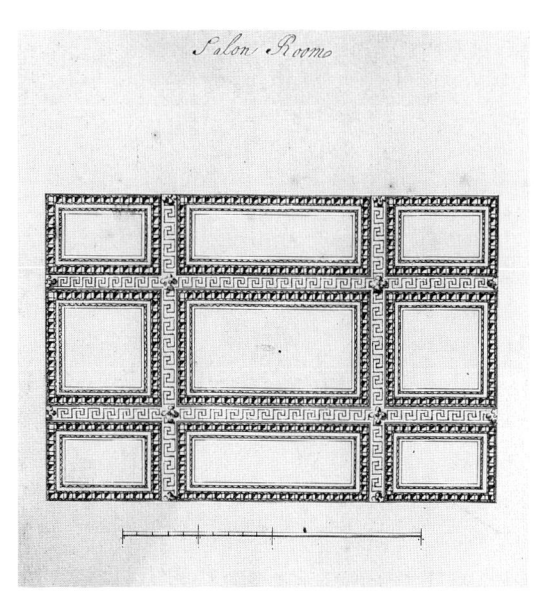

75
Design for the salon-ceiling of Richmond House, c. 1732, Lord Burlington

St. Paul's Cathedral, a view similar to the one that Canaletto captured in his painting *London: The Thames and the City of London from Richmond House*.

The ceilings depicted in the three drawings are similar to the beamed ceilings in the rooms of the *piano nobile* of the Villa at Chiswick, which, in turn, are based upon the ceilings in Jones's Queen's House, Greenwich, and Somerset Chapel in Somerset House, demolished to make way for William Chambers' new Somerset House. Burlington chose Jones' beamed ceiling because he understood

83

that it derived from the *soffitto veneziano*, a Venetian ceiling consisting of sumptuously decorated beams with oil paintings inserted into the panels between the beams. Jones introduced the *soffitto veneziano* to England,[46] and Burlington had seen it on his travels through northern Italy and, especially, in Venice and the Veneto.

The richness of these beamed ceilings in Richmond House is probably reflective of the overall sumptuousness of the interiors of the house. This contrast between exterior and interior is another hallmark of Burlington's architecture. It characterises the exteriors and interiors of Holkham Hall, Norfolk, the country seat of Thomas Coke, on the design for which Burlington exerted strong influence, and to a lesser extent characterised the Villa at Chiswick, where there is some forewarning, in the portico and pedimented windows, of the richness and grandeur that await on the interiors. Like much of Burlington's architectural theory and practice, the contrast between exterior and interior derives from Jones and is epitomised in a statement in his Roman Sketchbook of 1614, which Burlington owned:

For as outwardly every wise man carries a gravity in public places, where there is nothing else looked for yet inwardly has his imagination set free, and sometimes licentiously flying out, as nature herself does often times stravagantly, to delight, amuse us, sometimes move us to laughter, sometimes to contemplation and horror. So in Architecture the outward ornaments ought to be solid, proportional, according to the rules, masculine and unaffected. Whereas within cameras used by the ancients they varied and composed ornaments both of the house itself and the movable furniture within it [and they] are most commendable.[47]

A Design for Colonel James Gee's House

The only house outside London that Burlington designed was for Colonel James Gee and was to be built in the village of Bishop Burton in the East Riding of Yorkshire, not far from the market town of Beverly. Because of Burlington's inscription "for Col: Gee at Bishop Burton Yorkshire" on the drawing of the house, it has traditionally been thought that it was designed for Colonel William Gee (1699-1745).[48] Now it appears that the house in fact was designed for William's uncle, Colonel James Gee (1686-1751). James Gee was a member of an old, well established Yorkshire family and, like other members of his family, was a good friend of Burlington and his circle.[49]

The only information about Burlington's design is a drawing of the front elevation of the house by Flitcroft. (Fig. 76) The elevation is rather a pompous affair, more in keeping with a house in London than in the village of Bishop Burton. Indeed, when compared with the Gee family seat of High Hall, occupied by James's brother, Thomas, one can readily understand why the house was never built. (Fig. 77) On stylistic grounds, the elevation belongs to the early period of Burlington's architecture during the first part of the

76
Front elevation of Colonel James Gee's house, c. 1722, Lord Burlington

1720s and bears affinities with the Mountrath residence in London and with an early design for a front elevation of Tottenham Park, with its two-storey pedimented centrepiece. In 1722, James leased a small estate in Bishop Burton and may have intended to build a house on it. But, since a house already stood on the property, he may have changed his mind, put aside Burlington's design, and made Low Hall his residence.[50]

77
Samuel Buck's drawing of High Hill House, Bishop Burton, Yorkshire, c.1720

Conclusion

Burlington stood at the threshold of London's development into an eighteenth-century metropolis following the Peace of Utrecht in 1713. The great building boom that ensued continued throughout the century and saw London expand west along the Thames far beyond the City and the Inns of Court toward Whitehall and Westminster Abbey and, with the development of the great estates, along Piccadilly towards Hyde Park.

Did Burlington's architecture play a major role in defining eighteenth-century London? He really did not wield the power or influence that his architectural ideals and social position would have permitted. Although he opened a housing development behind Burlington House, he failed to assume architectural control over it and therefore forfeited a wonderful opportunity to make a major statement about urban design and taste. Then, too, his architectural production was very limited; of his ten designs for institutional buildings and residences, only half were erected. Certainly, his three houses were located on prime sites in the newly emerging London, in the Privy Garden of Whitehall and behind Burlington House. Nevertheless, they did not constitute a major contribution to London's urban environment. The exteriors of the Mountrath and Richmond houses were not very different from Campbell's London houses or from those designed by other architects. General Wade's town house, which was truly an innovation, had its Doric facade relegated to the garden elevation, away from the public eye. To be sure, the concept of the temple front did become a standard treatment for town residences, but not quite in the didactic, emphatic manner that Wade's town house exemplifies. Burlington's two institutional buildings that were erected, the Westminster Dormitory and the York Assembly Rooms, were uncompromising statements of his architectural principles, but they had no great progeny.

In fact, it is the elements of Burlington's architecture, rather than his architecture as a whole, that are his greatest contribution to Palladian town architecture. The Serliana and thermal windows became, through his efforts, leitmotifs of Palladian architecture in the town and the country. So, too, did the Venetian-style beamed ceiling, exemplified in Richmond House and probably in the town houses of Wade and Mountrath, become a standard fixture of the Palladian interior. On the other hand, Burlington's sophisticated use of Italianate rustication failed to make an impact on Palladian town architecture.

What was Burlington's vision? Of all the architects of his day, he was the most uncompromising in following his dream of joining England to the Continent and, specifically, to the classical tradition of the Mediterranean. Burlington took up where Jones left off, continuing an architecture of austere simplicity found in Jones' Tuscan portico on St. Paul's, Covent Garden, and on his decastyle Corinthian portico on the west front of St. Paul's Cathedral. Burlington continued the tradition of the rich, sumptuous, Baroque interior that contrasted with the simplicity of the exterior, a tradition established by Jones and derived from Venice and Palladio.

All this came at great cost to Burlington and to his patrons, most of whom were his friends and fellow peers. The freedom that his wealth and social position gave him also worked against him. To a certain extent, he needed the restraints of client demands and restrictions of economic necessity to balance his strong intellectual and theoretical approach to architecture. With some of his designs, he did, indeed, fail to achieve what Pope claimed for him: "You show us Rome was glorious, not profuse, / And pompous buildings once were things of Use."[51] Pope admonished others for permitting the "rules of art" to dominate to the exclusion of "Good Sense," but, in fairness, this failing applies to Burlington in some instances.[52] Burlington probably lost the commission for the Chichester Council House and Pulteney's London house in part because of his intellectual devotion to his ideas. Certainly, he failed to meet the one request his friend General Wade made of him, to design a space large enough to hang Rubens' cartoon of *The Calydonian Boar*.

Idealistic, intellectual and sometimes pedantic and impractical, Burlington attempted to establish the standards of classical architecture for England and, in the process, created an architecture that is intellectually stimulating and visually provocative.

Notes

Introduction

1. Aikman started the portrait in the early autumn and completed it by 2 November, as indicated by his letter to his cousin, Sir John Clerk of Penicuik. "I have done a pict of my Lord and Lady Burlington upon one cloath which has great applause. The Gentleman for whom they satt payd me 20 guineas tho the cloath was under the syze of a half-length and has commissioned a fine frame from Paris." William Aikman to Sir John Clerk, 2 Nov 1723, GD18/4589, Clerk of Penicuik Papers, Scottish Record Office, Edinburgh. I am grateful to Dr. Iain Brown for supplying me with this quotation.

2. Colen Campbell, Introduction, *Vitruvius Britannicus . . .*, I (London, 1715).

3. Ibid.

4. Since 1894, Burlington's drawings collection has been divided between the Royal Institute of British Architects, London, and the Devonshire Collection, Chatsworth.

5. Burlington's library is now housed at Chatsworth.

Chapter 1

Burlington's Architectural Education

1. There is no mention in Burlington's Grand Tour Account Book that he took the time to study architecture. Unlike Coke, he does not appear to have studied architecture with a tutor; nor did he purchase architectural treatises or take trips through Italy to study architecture as Coke and Kent did. Burlington's Grand Tour account book is in the Chiswick Archives at Chatsworth.

2. Burrel Massingberd to William Kent, 5 July 1714, from London, Massingberd-Kent Correspondence, 2MM B/19A, Lincolnshire County Council, Lincolnshire Archives, The Castle, Lincoln.

3. John Macky, *Journey through England in Familiar Letters from a Gentleman Here to a Friend Abroad*, I (London, 1714), p. 125.

4. Thomas Whately, "An Essay on the Different Natural Situations of Gardens," in *Observations on Modern Gardening, and Laying Out of Pleasure-Grounds, Parks, Farms, Ridings . . .* (London, 1801), p. 153. Horace Walpole was responsible for annotating the second edition of Whately's *Observations*.

5. Campbell, *Vitruvius Britannicus* III (1725), p. 8.

6. R. T. Gunter, ed., *The Architecture of Roger Pratt . . . from His Notebooks* (1928; reprint ed., New York, 1979), pp. 23-24.

7. Ibid., p. 24.

8. Dr. James Hay to the Countess of Northamptonhire, 27 December 1719, N.S., from Grenoble, cited by Peter McKay, "The Grand Tour of the Hon. Charles Compton," *Northamptonshire Past & Present* VII (Northampton, 1986), p. 250.

9. Burlington's annotated copy of Palladio's treatise is in the library at Chatsworth.

10. Andrea Palladio, *Fabbriche' Antiche Disegnate' Da Andrea Palladio Vicentino* (London, 1730), All Intendente Lettore.

11. Ibid. For the probable publication date in the late 1740s for the *Fabbriche*, see Eileen Harris, *British Architectural Books and Writers 1556-1785* (Cambridge, 1990), pp. 348-52.

12. Messers Graham and Collier Joynt Accounts, fol. 2, s.v., 4 May 1720, Disbursement of Funds Section, 28 Ap 1720 to 21 May 1721, Chiswick Archives, Chatsworth.

13. Ibid., fol. 36, s.v. 7 Ap 1721.

14 Macky, *Journey through England*, I (1724), p. 72.

15 *Voiage d'Angleterre, d Hollande et de Flandre fait in année 1728*, fol. 137-38, 86 NN2, National Art Library, Victoria and Albert Museum, London.

Chapter 2

The Institutional Designs and Buildings

1 Arthur T. Bolton and H. Duncan Hendrey, eds., *Wren Society*, XI (Oxford, 1934), p. 38

2 Ibid.

3 G. F. Russell Barker and Allen H. Stenning, *The Record of Old Westminsters* I (1928; London, 1963), p. 113.

4 The foundation stone was laid by Burlington on 21 April 1722, and the inscription reads: "Posuit felicibus (faxit Deus) Auspiciis Ricardus Comes de Burlington, architectus, 7 Kal Maii 1722" *Wren Society*, p. 41. All relevant documentation and drawings have been published in volume 11 of *The Wren Society*.

5 Howard Colvin, *A Biographical Dictionary of British Architects 1600-1840* (1954; London, 1978), pp. 309-10.

6 Since Burlington's day, the dormitory has undergone drastic changes and alterations. In 1847, the arcade was walled and given fenestration, and at about the same time the blind niches on the first floor were given fenestration. Then, in May 1941, a fire caused by bombing gutted the interiors, leaving only the outer walls standing.

7 John Summerson, *Georgian London* (Harmondsworth, 1969), p. 119.

8 Andrea Palladio, *I Quattro Libri Dell'Architettura di Andrea Palladio* (Venice, 1570), Book I, pp. 28-36.

9 Burlington's annotation about the cloister concerns the composition of the Ionic window frames on the first floor. This annotation is on an interleaf page after the title page of Burlington's copy of the 1601 edition of *I Quattro Libri*,

10 Brian Scragg, *Sevenoaks School: A History* (Bath, 1993), pp. 13-18.

11 Ibid., p. 52.

12 Ibid., pp. 22, 52-53.

13 Leslie Stephen and Sidney Lee, *The Dictionary of National Biography* VI (1921-22), pp. 1186-87; John Lodge, *The Peerage of Ireland* . . . I (London, 1754), pp. 294-96.

14 Inigo Jones, *The Designs of Inigo Jones . . .*, II (London, 1727), Plate 53.

15 Scragg, *Sevenoaks School*, p. 45.

16 Mark Girouard describes three types of almshouse layouts, but Burlington's design does not fit any of them precisely, although it is closest to the single range of almshouse type. See Mark Girouard, *The English Town: A History* (New Haven, 1990), pp. 57-63.

17 Dan Cruickshank and Neil Burton, *Life in the Georgian City* (London, 1990), p. 139.

18 Palladio, *I Quattro Libri* (1570), Book II, p. 55.

19 James Spershott, "Memoirs of the City of Chichester and Its Environs," in David J. Butler, *The Two Plans of Chichester 1595-1898* (Chichester, 1972), p. 9.

20 Ibid.

21 L. F. Salzman, ed., *The Victorian History of the Counties of England: Sussex* III (1939), p. 89.

22 George Vertue, *The Note Books of G. Vertue Relating to Artists and Collections in England*, Walpole Society, XXVI (Oxford, 1989), p. 144.

23 This is definitely the second of the two council-house designs. On the verso of the sheet containing the floor plan of the first floor, Burlington wrote, "for the D of Richmond for a towne house at Chichester." Furthermore, there is a reference to a town house in Richmond's letter to Burlington of 29 June 1730 asking for "the Towne House" design, so that Richmond could take it with him to Chichester on Friday, 3 July, "where I dare not go without a plan" (Richmond to Burlington, 29 June 1730, 201.0, Chiswick Archives, Chatsworth).

24 This annotation is on the interleaf page after the title page of Burlington's copy of the 1601 edition of *I Quattro Libri*.

25 Palladio, *I Quattro Libri* (1570), Book I, p. 52.

26 Richmond to Burlington, 22 June 1730, 201.1, Chiswick Archives, Chatsworth.

27 Richmond to Burlington, 29 June 1730, 201.0, Chiswick Archives, Chatsworth.

28 Terry Friedman, *James Gibbs* (New Haven, 1984), pp. 213-20.

29 *Designs of Inigo Jones and Others* (London, 1731), verso of title page.

30 St. George's Hospital Minute Book, 19 Oct 1733-31 Dec 1735, fols. 29, 112, 138, 169, London.

31 Girouard, *English Town*, pp. 127-40.

32 Colvin, *A Biographical Dictionary of British Architects 1600-1840*, pp. 860-61.

33 Copy of a letter from the directors to Burlington, 4 May 1730, York Assembly Rooms Minute Book and Account Books, fol. 7, s.v., 4 May 1730, 1729-58, York City Record Office, York (hereafter cited as York Minute and Account Books).

34. Ibid.

35. Ibid.

36. Ibid., fol. 8, s.v., 13 May 1730.

37. Gladys Scott Thomson, ed., *Letters of a Grandmother 1732-35. Being the Correspondence of Sarah, Duchess of Marlborough with her Granddaughter, Diana, Duchess of Bedford* (London, 1943), p. 41.

38. Copy of a letter from Burlington to the directors of the York Assembly Rooms, York Minute and Account Books, fol. 11, s.v., 31 Oct 1730.

39. Ibid., fol. 12, s.v., 19 Jan 1731.

40. Ibid., copy of a letter from Daniel Garrett to Mr. Travers, 18 Dec 1731, fol. 45, s.v., 18 Dec. 1731. Garrett wrote a letter outlining the dimensions of the doors and windows for the Great Assembly Room.

41. I have used the ground plan illustrated in Francis Drake's *Eboracum*, for it is accurate, whereas Flitcroft's ground plan is a penultimate ground plan [Francis Drake, *Eboracum: Or the History and Antiquities of the City of York from Its Original to the Present Time* (London, 1736), p. 338].

42. *I Quattro Libri* (1570), Book I, pp. 37-43.

43. Album 26A, Devonshire Collections, Chatsworth.

44. York Minute and Account Books, fol. 62, s.v., 7 Aug 1732.

45. Thomson, *Letters of a Grandmother*, p. 41.

46. Only the two thermal windows aligned with the columnar screens in the rooms to either side of the Great Assembly Room have survived. It is not clear if any of the other fenestration intended for the side elevations was executed. The Assembly Rooms have undergone drastic changes since Burlington's day. Major alterations began in 1828 with the replacement of Burlington's stone portico with J. P. Pritchett's shallow tetrastyle portico. This was followed in 1859 by the pulling down of the side walls between the Great Assembly Room and two side rooms. The York Corporation acquired the building in 1925, and in 1951 the restoration of the assembly rooms was complete. See *Royal Commission on Historical Monuments. An Inventory of the Historical Monuments in the City of York: The Central Area*, V (Leicester, 1981), p. 100.

47. York Minute and Account Books, fol. 8, s.v., 11 May 1730; fols. 15 & 16, s.v., 25 Feb 1731.

48. Thomson, *Letters*, p. 58.

49. York Minute and Account Books, fol. 61, s.v., 4 Aug 1732.

50. Ibid., fol. 63, s.v., 18 Aug 1732. Burlington was indeed a generous contributor to the assembly rooms building fund. He, his wife, two of his daughters, his mother, and his sister and brother-in-law, Lord and Lady Bruce, as well as the Savile relatives Sir George and Lady Savile contributed a total of £400 (see Drake, *Eboracum*, appen. 54 & 55). In addition to this financial support, Burlington donated a large chandelier for the centre of the Great Assembly Room and twelve other, smaller chandeliers for the room (*The Monthly Intelligencer*, July 1732, p. 873).

51. Burlington's annotation is on the interleaf page following the titlepage of the 1601 edition of *I Quattro Libri*.

52. *I Quattro Libri* (1570), Book II, pp. 41-42.

53. Ibid., Book III, pp. 38-39.

54. York Minute and Account Books, fol. 61, s.v., 4 Aug 1732.

55. Thomson, *Letters*, p. 41.

56. Drake, Dedication, *Eboracum*.

57. Burlington to Lady Burlington, 127.3, Chiswick Archives, Chatsworth.

58. York Minute and Account Books, fol. 138, s.v., 3 March 1735.

59. Ibid.

60. Ibid., fol. 9, s.v., 5 June 1730; fol. 122, s.v., 4 June 1735. For a complete history of the transaction, see Drake *Eboracum*, appen. 59-61. For a building history of the Piazza, see Ian H. Goodall, "Lord Burlington's York 'Piazza,'" in the *York Georgian Society's Annual Report* (1970), pp. 22-38.

61. Ibid.

62. Ibid., fol. 137. s.v., 20 Oct 1735.

63. Burlington's Piazza was demolished in 1859.

64. For a history of the evolution of assembly rooms, see Girouard, *The English Town*, pp. 127-44.

Chapter 3

THE TOWN HOUSES

1. F. H. W. Sheppard, ed., *The Survey of London. The Parish of St. James Westminster. Part Two. North of Piccadilly*, XXXII (London, 1963), p. 446.

2. Ibid., pp. 539-42; Governors Minute Book for the Burlington School for Girls, s.v., 29 May and 6, 7, 10, 26 August 1719, The Burlington-Danes School, Hammersmith

3. For a list of those who owned or rented property in Burlington's development, see *Survey of London*, pp. 546-65.

4. Ibid., p. 501.

5. *Vitruvius Britannicus*, III, [6], Subscribers, s.v., W; *Designs of Inigo Jones*, I, Subscribers, s.v., W.

6. Verso of the last blank page of the Book of Hours, Devonshire Collections, Chatsworth.

7   *A Catalogue of . . . Pictures . . . of the late Gen. Wade*, Christie's, 19 April 1785; *A Catalogue of , , , Pictures . . . of John Wade . . . originally collected by his Father, Field Marshal Wade*, Christie's, 27 March 1797.

8   Benjamin Boyce, *The Benevolent Man: A Life of Ralph Allen* (Cambridge, Mass., 1967), pp. 37-39.

9   Since none of the extant drawings is dated, I have relied on the date of 1723 given by Campbell, *Vitruvius Britannicus*, III [7] and Plate 10.

10 Burlington's copy of Palladio's *I Quattro Libri*, Book II, p. 14.

11 Bruce Allsopp, *Inigo Jones on Palladio*, I (Newcastle upon Tyne, 1970), pp. 21-23 and II, Book II, pp. 12-15.

12 Tim Knox and Todd Longstaffe-Gowan, "A Town Garden Design for 29 Old Burlington Street, Westminster," *Georgian Group Journal* (1991): 36-40.

13 *Survey of London*, p. 504.

14 Ibid. In 1823, Wade's town house was converted into the Burlington Hotel.

15 "Town House Design," pp. 38-40.

16 Ibid., p. 39.

17 *Survey of London*, p. 499, Fig. 92 (the c.1773 plan of the property).

18 Ibid.; *Vitruvius Britannicus*, III, Plate 10. The ground- and first-floor plans for Wade's town house in *Vitruvius Britannicus* are virtually identical.

19 Horace Walpole to George Montague, 18 May 1748, Horace Walpole, *Private Correspondence of Horace Walpole, Earl of Oxford* (London, 1820), p. 172.

20 Ibid.

21 [Horace Walpole], *Aedes Walpolianae: Or a Description of the Collection of Pictures at Houghton Hall . . . the Seat of . . .Robert Walpole* (London, 1752, 2d ed.), p. 80.

22 Walpole, *Private Correspondence*, I, p. 172.

23 Ibid.

24 [James Ralph], *A Critical Review of the Publick Buildings, Statues and Ornaments in, and about London and Westminster* (London, 1734; reprinted., 1971), pp. 103-04.

25 Joseph Addison, *The Spectator*, no. 415, 26 June 1712, ed. Donald F. Bond, III (Oxford, 1965), pp. 553-58.

26 Alexander Pope, *Alexander Pope: Selected Poetry and Prose* (New York, 1965). p. 205.

27 *The Peerage of Ireland* . . . , p. 312.

28 *Survey of London*, p. 505. The Mountrath house was demolished in 1935 along with General Wade's town house. For a thorough history of the ownership of the house, see *Survey of London*, pp. 505-08.

29 *Designs of Inigo Jones*, I, Plate 57.

30 The only instance of such an aedicular treatment is on the windows of the front elevation for the design of Lord Lincoln's Villa (Boy [20], 2, Royal Institute of British Architects Drawings Collection, London.

31 See John Harris, *Catalogue of the Drawings Collection of the Royal Institute of British Architects: Colen Campbell* (Farnborough, 1973), Fig. 58.

32 *Dictionary of National Biography*, XVI, pp. 471-78.

33 *Designs of Inigo Jones*, II, Plate 12.

34 *Survey of London*, pp. 27, 117-18.

35 Treasury Chambers, Whitehall, P.R.O., T. 54/21, fol. 95.

36 Ibid., P.R.O., T. 55/2, fols. 422-23 & fol. 425.

37 Receipts & Payments by Robert Sedgwick on Account of His Grace the Duke Richmond, 12 May 1733 to 29 Sept 1734, fol. 92, s.v., 12 May 1733, Goodwood Ms., 126, West Sussex Record Office, Chichester.

38 Ibid., fol. 93, s.v., 19 May 1733.

39 *Life in the Georgian City*, pp. 54-55.

40 Katharine Baetjer and J. G. Links, *Canaletto* (New York, 1989), p. 11, Fig. 4.

41 Ibid., pp. 233-36.

42 Henry B. Wheatley, *London Past and Present* . . . , III (London, 1891), p. 162.

43 The second Duke's residence was destroyed by a fire on 21 Dec. 1791 (*Survey of London*, XIII, p. 248).

44 T. P. Connor, "Architecture and Planting at Goodwood, 1723-1750," in *Sussex Archaeological Collections* CXVII (Lewes, 1979), p. 187; Edward Croft-Murray, *Decorative Painting in England 1537-1837*, II (London, 1970), p. 234.

45 Richmond to Burlington, 201.5, Chiswick Archives, Chatsworth.

46 Juergen Schulz, *Venetian Painted Ceilings of the Renaissance* (Berkeley, 1968), pp. 52-53.

47 Inigo Jones, Roman Sketchbook, 1614, s.v., 20 Jan. 1614, Devonshire Collections, Chatsworth.

48 David Neave, "High and Low Halls, Bishop Burton," *The Georgian Society of Yorkshire*, no. 6 (1979).

49 Ibid.

50 Ibid.

51 Pope, *Selected Poetry*, p. 206.

52 Ibid.